515901

G000041887

PERSONAL CHOICE

Ambrose Heath

PERSONAL CHOICE

Introduction by Arabella Boxer

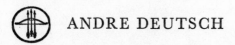 ANDRE DEUTSCH

First published 1971 by
André Deutsch Limited, 105 Great Russell Street,
London WC1

Copyright © 1971 by André Deutsch Ltd
All Rights Reserved

Printed in Great Britain by
Ebenezer Baylis and Son Ltd
The Trinity Press,
Worcester, and London

ISBN 0 233 96251 4

Contents

Introduction

Ambrose Heath held for many years a special place among food writers, and this book makes an appropriate end to his work. Climax would be too dramatic a word to describe it, for in spite of having written more than seventy books, his writing was always marked by its modesty and lack of any pretension, a quality rare among writers on food and drink.

As a young man he was much influenced by Marcel Boulestin, and even in this last book, written forty years later, one can still see the similarity in their attitude. Boulestin wrote about food of an enviable simplicity, and the dishes he described are not to be confused with those to be found in his restaurant, which belong to a totally different tradition and which he would never have recommended for home cooking.

In spite of this influence, Ambrose Heath has always endeared himself to me as the most English of cookery writers. I do not mean to say that he wrote only about classic English dishes; on the contrary he created a sort of cuisine of his own, making use of indigenous materials in ways especially relevant to this country. He used ideas and impressions freely from other countries, but always with understanding of their application to English food.

More than any other writer, he seemed very aware of the seasons, and closely in touch with nature. His first book, *Good Food*, was written in the form of a monthly calendar using food in season, as was also my favourite of Boulestin's books, *What Shall We Have Today?* It is to writers such as these that perhaps we owe the most, those who remind us of the value of purity in food, of simple ingredients cooked in appropriate and wholesome ways, rather than those who constantly urge us to experiment with exotic dishes in their search for new gastronomic experience. As Ambrose Heath himself says in the introduction to one of his books, his aim is 'Beautifully cooked simple dishes, whose attractiveness lies in the perfection of their cooking . . . good food perfectly cooked and simply presented, without unnecessary trappings and superfluous garnishes. . . .'

I feel sure that all admirers of Ambrose Heath will welcome this book; the recipes are his own favourites from the thousands he had tried, and as the distilled essence of so much work are truly characteristic of his tastes.

ARABELLA BOXER

SOUPS

CABBAGE SOUP

The full-blooded result of the usual wedding of cabbage and pickled pork is what we think of first when this soup is mentioned. But there is a milder and, to some, more attractive form which is given below, although to be sure it does not provide a bonus of cold pork for next day's breakfast.

1 white cabbage (small)
water
1 potato
3 level teaspoons butter

1 quart milk
salt and pepper
grated cheese

Boil the shredded cabbage in salted water for half an hour, then add the peeled and sliced potato, and boil half an hour longer. Drain off the water, mash up the vegetables roughly with a fork, and add butter, milk, salt and pepper to taste. Stir carefully over a low heat for ten minutes, and serve with grated cheese handed separately. Serves 4.

CELERIAC SOUP

A creamy soup from the turnip-rooted celery makes a pleasant change from the usual celery soup and affords the enterprising guest with an opportunity of guessing what gives it that subtle difference.

1 lb celeriac	1 quart white stock
water	*croûtons*
1 oz butter	cream (optional)
2 potatoes (medium size)	

Chop up finely carefully pared celeriac, and blanch it in boiling water. Then drain it and cook it for a little in the butter. Add the potatoes also finely chopped and after a few minutes the stock. Simmer until the vegetables are tender, pass through a very fine sieve and let the result reduce very slowly for half an hour. Add cream if you like, but certainly have fried *croûtons* of bread with it. Serves 4.

CREAM OF BARLEY SOUP

A regular nursery soup, and jolly good too. Since retasting this smooth creaminess when I was old enough to know better, it has become a firm favourite.

2 oz pearl barley	1 quart white stock
1 oz butter	nutmeg (optional)
1 onion (small)	1 egg-yolk
1 carrot (small)	*croûtons*
1 stick celery (or celery salt)	

Wash the pearl barley, and then blanch it. In the butter *sauté* the onion, carrot and celery (or add celery salt later), the vegetables all cut small, and then add the barley and stock. Cook gently for a couple of hours, and then strain. Season, if you like, with a touch of nutmeg, and bind with egg-yolk. Reheat without boiling, and serve with *croûtons* of fried bread. Serves 4.

CREME VICHYSSOISE

This form of Leek and Potato soup made its name in the twentieth century when it became a fashionable first course in summertime. It has been widely adopted in this country, where some are induced by the

climate to serve it hot in the appropriate seasons, but it then loses the
distinction which the novelty of coldness gives it.

2 oz butter	1 sprig parsley (small)
2 leeks	1 potato
1 onion (small)	salt and pepper
1 pint chicken stock (or diluted chicken bouillon cube)	1 teacup heavy cream chives
1 stick celery (or celery salt)	

Melt the butter in a saucepan, add the finely cut white part of the leeks,
the minced onion, and stew very slowly until quite soft but not at all
browned. Now add chicken stock, celery, parsley, the thinly sliced potato
and a seasoning of salt and pepper to taste, using celery salt if celery is
unobtainable. Cook on until the potato is tender, then rub the whole
thing through a fine sieve. Serve in a china or glass bowl and, just before
serving, stir in the cream. Chopped chives should be handed with the
soup, or sprinkled over the top of separate helpings. It should be as
cold, and therefore as refreshing, as possible. Serves 4.

CREOLE SOUP

This is the most pleasant way I know of making a soup of tomatoes and
green pepper, and it should be tried immediately the latter become
available in our greengrocers' shops. If you have a definite dislike for
vinegar, its addition is not absolutely essential, but the presence of the
horseradish is, I think.

2 tablespoons onion	salt and pepper
3 tablespoons green sweet peppers	cayenne
2 oz butter	grated horseradish
1½ oz flour	1 dash vinegar (optional)
1 lb tomatoes	2 tablespoons cooked macaroni
1 quart brown stock	rings

Fry the chopped onion and green sweet peppers in the butter for five
minutes. Mix in the flour, then the quartered tomatoes, stock, and
simmer for about half an hour. Pass through a sieve, and season highly
with salt, pepper, and cayenne. Some people add a dash of vinegar
and a little grated horseradish just before serving, and garnish it with
rings of cooked macaroni. Serves 4.

CUCUMBER SOUP

A delicious light summer soup when cucumbers are plentiful. The ridge ones will do for this, provided they are young and not too seedy.

1 cucumber (medium)	grated nutmeg
1 oz butter	2 egg-yolks
2 onions (small)	1 tablespoon cream (approximately)
water	
salt and pepper	*croûtons* (optional)
cayenne	chervil (optional)

Cut the peeled cucumber into thin slices, and toss these in butter for a few minutes. Keep them warm while in the same pan you fry very lightly the sliced onions. Take out the onions and add them to the cucumber in a saucepan, pouring over them both enough boiling water – *not* stock – to make the right amount of soup after it has eventually boiled away by a quarter. Season with salt, pepper, a little grated nutmeg and a tiny pinch of cayenne pepper, and simmer for about half an hour, when the proper reduction should have been made. Then bind with the egg-yolks beaten into the cream, and serve if you like with tiny fried bread *croûtons*. Some like to sprinkle it at the very end with a little chopped chervil. Serves 4.

CURRIED FISH SOUP

This soup is suitable for all those who like currying fish, and they will turn for a companion dish to CURRIED PRAWNS on page 28, about its easiest manifestation. Some like a slightly larger squeeze of lemon at the end.

1 lb fresh haddock	½ oz curry powder
2 oz butter	2 oz flour
1 apple	salt and pepper
2 onions	lemon juice
1 teaspoon mixed herbs	2 oz cooked rice
1 quart fish stock (or water)	

Skin, bone, and cut the haddock into small pieces. Brown them in the butter with the peeled diced apple, the onions, chopped, and the mixed herbs. After ten minutes add the hot fish stock, bring to the boil, and simmer for half an hour. Now mix the curry powder and flour with a little water, and stir these into the soup, bringing it to the boil again and simmering for another half-hour. Then rub it all through a sieve, re-heat, season with salt, pepper, and a little lemon juice, and serve, handing hot boiled rice separately. Serves 4.

FLANDERS LEEK SOUP

The presence of sorrel gives this soup an unexpected charm, as does the rather rough treatment it receives from the wooden spoon. The result of an impromptu raid on the kitchen garden, I should think, spinach being substituted for the sorrel for the benefit of those who dislike or fear that vegetable's acidity.

1 handful sorrel (or spinach) leaves	salt and pepper
2 handfuls chervil	1 oz butter
6 leeks (medium)	1 sprig fresh or ½ teaspoon dried savory (or basil)
2 lettuces (or endives)	6 potatoes (medium)
2 pints water	

Cut up the prepared sorrel (or spinach) leaves, the chervil, leeks (the white part only) and the lettuces (or endives), according to the season. Cook these in enough salted water to make your soup, adding a nice piece of butter, pepper, the savory or basil and the potatoes cut in quarters. Cook for four or five hours on a low fire and serve the soup as it is, crushing the potatoes coarsely with a wooden spoon. Serves 4.

GREEN PEAPOD SOUP

I have never made this elegant and economical soup with peas bought from a shop, as I have a sneaking idea (probably wrong) that they may have been sprayed with an insecticide, so my advice is to use peas from your own garden, which will reward you when it comes to stripping off the inside skin, owing to their freshness. It is indeed one of the most delicious of pea soups and will grace any meal at which it is served.

1 quart peapods	salt and pepper
2 quarts water	sugar
1 sprig mint	½ pint milk
1 lettuce (small)	1–2 tablespoons cream
1 sprig parsley	small peas
1 onion (small)	

Peapods make a nice light soup, satisfying both to the palate and the pocket. Wash the peapods well, and pull off the inside skin. Put them into boiling water with the mint, lettuce, parsley and onion. Cook all together until the vegetables are tender, then rub through a fine sieve. Boil the soup up again, season it with pepper, salt, and a pinch of sugar, and add the milk. A spoonful or two of cream will help to enrich this very cheap soup, and a few little peas will act as a garnish. Serves 4.

HUNGARIAN ONION SOUP

This is a forceful soup in the preparation of which only the very best paprika pepper should be used. This sweet pepper varies a good deal in this country so it is as well to be armed with what to my mind is second to none. This is the *Hungarian Kotanyi Paprika Edelsüss Spezial.* The same remarks as far as the pepper is concerned apply to GOULASH OF BEEF on page 49.

2 onions	2 tomatoes
2 tablespoons lard	salt
1 teaspoon paprika pepper	1 handful noodles (or spaghetti,
1½ quarts stock	or rice)

Slice the onions thinly, and stew them in the lard until they are golden-brown, adding towards the end the paprika pepper. Pour over the stock, and the tomatoes cut in quarters, season with salt, and boil for a quarter of an hour. Strain and serve with noodles, spaghetti, or rice cooked in the soup at the last. Serves 4.

LETTUCE SOUP

One of the most delicate soups of summer with its enrichment of egg and cream, and something to set your visitors talking. For kitchen-gardeners a good way of using up your early-bolting lettuces.

2 lettuces	water
1 handful spinach	salt and pepper
½ oz butter	1 egg-yolk
1 handful parsley	cream

Cut the equivalent of two lettuces in outside leaves and the spinach into strips, and stew them with a little butter and the chopped parsley until they are quite soft. Then add enough hot water to make your soup, season with salt and pepper, bring to the boil, and simmer for about three-quarters of an hour. This soup should be served as it is, thickened with an egg-yolk beaten in a little cream. The lettuce heart may be used in a salad. Serves 4.

MUSSEL SOUP

The delicate flavour of mussels was never better than in this soup, which offers all the pleasure of *moules marinière* without that tiresome fumbling with the shells. There is another rather good recipe for *Potage Vermicelle Granvillaise*, but you must look up Madame Prunier's Fish Cookery Book for this.

1½ pints mussels	1 leek
1 teacup water	1 tomato
2 onions (small)	salt and pepper
½ clove garlic	3 tablespoons rice
1 bayleaf	1 pinch saffron (optional)
olive oil	

Scrape the mussels, clean them well under running cold water, and put them into a stewpan with a good teacupful of water, one onion, crushed garlic, and a bayleaf. Cook them on a quick heat until they open, then take them out, and decant their liquid through a cloth into another pan. Take the mussels from their shells, remove any weed from them and keep them warm in a pan or bowl with a cloth over it. Now stew in a little olive oil the white part of the leek, the other onion and the skinned tomato, all chopped finely, and moisten with the liquor from the mussels. Add

another scant pint of water, and season with salt and pepper. Bring this
to the boil, and cook in it the rice adding, if you can, a tiny pinch of
saffron. When the rice is tender, add the mussels, cook gently for another
five minutes, and serve as hot as possible. Serves 4.

ONION SOUP

Whether one thinks, when Onion Soup is mentioned, of a specific for a
cold in the head or a visit to *Les Halles* in Paris, it is sure to have been
made on some such lines as this. Last thing at night it is the most
wonderful food in the world – so long as your bed companion is an
imbiber too. . . . And for those who are looking for a dainty soup which
combines the subtle flavour of chicken giblets with tiny onions the
BUTTON ONION SOUP below will amply fill the bill.

4 large onions	sugar
1 quart water	grated cheese (or cubes of toasted
1½ oz butter	or fried bread sprinkled with
salt and pepper	cheese)

Cut the onions into thin slices and cook them in butter until they are
golden but not browned. Now pour in enough hot water so that when
the soup is sufficiently reduced, the right quantity will remain; then
cook on, adding a little salt, a pinch of sugar and plenty of freshly
ground black pepper, until this reduction has been achieved. Serve with
grated cheese, or with small cubes of toast or fried bread first sprinkled
with cheese and then browned in the oven or under the grill. Serves 4.

Button Onion Soup

1 handful button onions (same size)	½ teaspoon sugar (small)
butter (or chicken dripping)	1½ pints chicken stock
	salt and pepper

Skin the little onions and fry them lightly in a very little butter or
chicken dripping without browning them. Now add the sugar and fry
on, rolling the pan, until the onions are golden. Then add your chicken
stock, with salt and a little pepper, and boil for a quarter of an hour.
Serve just as it is. Serves 4.

PEASANT SOUP

A French *Soupe Paysanne* containing several vegetables makes good ammunition against winter-time.

2 carrots	parsley
2 onions	1 clove
2 tomatoes	peppercorns
2 leeks	salt
2 potatoes	2½ pints water
1 turnip (small)	1–2 tablespoons cream (optional)
2 oz butter	1–2 egg-yolks (optional)

Slice up the carrots, onions, tomatoes, leeks, potatoes and turnip, and let them stew for a while in a little butter. Now add a few sprigs of parsley, the clove, a few peppercorns, salt, and enough hot water to make the quantity of soup you want after allowing for reduction. Boil for about an hour, and rub the whole thing through a sieve. Now serve it as it is or bind it with a spoonful or two of cream and, if you like, an egg-yolk or two as well.

PORK AND SPLIT PEA SOUP

A steaming meal in itself. Rather more flippantly from the South of France comes a *Soupe des Noces*, invigorating enough for the wedding-guests to bring noisily to the marital bedside half-way through the proceedings.

½ pint split peas	4 onions
2 quarts water	celery salt
salt	2 oz butter
2 pig's trotters	

Soak the split peas in two quarts of water overnight, and then cook them slowly for two hours in the same water, salted. Pass through a fine sieve, and in this liquid cook the prepared pig's trotters for an hour. Now add the onions, celery salt, butter, and cook again until the onions are done. Serve as it is, if possible in the earthen casserole in which the soup was cooked. Serves 4.

POTAGE SANTE

The creamy white haricot bean soup which used to be sold under this name in Soho restaurants in my youth some sixty years ago was always garnished with small short strips of what we fondly supposed was sorrel but more likely was spinach. An excellent soup, but not so good as the SORREL SOUP (see page 19) we learned to drink some years later at the Hind's Head at Bray in Berkshire under the tutelage of my old friend, Barry Neame, a most delicious amalgam of sorrel, water and egg which gives the lie to anyone who contends that the most excellent soups must always be difficult and expensive.

3 potatoes (medium)	2 tablespoons sorrel leaves
salt	cream (optional)
water	1 egg-yolk (optional)
1½ pints white stock	butter

Peel the potatoes, quarter them, and cook them quickly in salted water. When they are soft, drain them, rub them through a fine sieve, and mix them with the stock. Have ready the thinly sliced sorrel leaves just 'melted' in butter, add them to the soup, and bind with cream or egg-yolk (or both), finishing with a few tiny bits of butter. Serves 4.

POTAGE SOLFERINO

The nineteenth-century craze for naming dishes after events spread in the Emperor Napoleon's time to commemoration of victories in the field. The Spanish allusion is contained in the nuance of its tomato flavour. A very pleasant and delicate soup.

1 onion (small)	½ clove garlic
2 leeks (optional)	flour
1 oz butter	steamed potato balls
1½ pints water	cooked or tinned French or runner
salt	beans
½ lb tomatoes	cooked carrot balls
¼ lb potatoes	

Cut up the onion and, when available, the white part of the leeks, and stew them without browning in half the butter. Add a pint and a half of lightly salted water and bring to the boil. Now put in the tomatoes and the potatoes cut in slices. Add also the garlic: its flavour will not be

too pronounced. Cover and simmer for half an hour or until the potatoes
are done, then rub through a sieve, diluting with a little more water, if
necessary. Bind with a little flour and butter if you wish, and serve
garnished with tiny steamed balls of potato and lozenges of cooked or
tinned French or runner beans, or little balls of cooked carrot. It
should be thickish-thin. Serves 4.

SORREL SOUP

½ lb sorrel	salt
1 oz butter	1 pinch sugar
1 tablespoon flour	2 eggs
1 quart water	

Pick over the sorrel leaves, removing the ribs and damaged leaves,
chop them up coarsely, and stew them slowly with a small piece of butter
in a covered pan for twenty minutes. Do not be disturbed at the change
their colour will undergo, they will taste just as good. Sprinkle over the
flour, and cook this a little. Now moisten with just over a quart of hot
water, and season with salt and a pinch of sugar. Cover, and boil gently
for a quarter of an hour. Now beat up the eggs and mix them with the
soup, pouring them through a strainer. The soup must not boil, of
course, after the eggs have been added. Serves 4.

SOUPE AUX CHOUX

1 piece pickled pork (or some	1 carrot
bacon bones)	1 turnip (small)
2½ pints water	1 white cabbage
parsley	pepper
thyme	garlic
bayleaf	streaky bacon

To be at its best it should be made with the water in which some pickled
pork has been boiled, but an excellent imitation can be made by boiling
some mild bacon bones in the water and using this instead, but do not
use too many, or it will be too salt. They should be boiled with a
bouquet of parsley, thyme and bayleaf, and when the water is flavoured
and the bones and bouquet are removed have ready the carrot and
turnip cut in little pieces and the white cabbage finely shredded. Add

these to the boiling liquid, with a little pepper to taste. Cook for an hour and a half and then throw in some finely chopped parsley, a little garlic, and a few thin strips of streaky bacon. Finish cooking for half an hour. Serves 4.

SOUPE DES NOCES

1 onion (large)	salt and pepper
6 tomatoes	1 tablespoon *vermicelli*
1½ oz lard	toast
1½ pints water	

Nothing could be simpler or more delicious in its way. Fry the minced onion and quartered tomatoes in a little lard, then put them in a stewpan with the water, and a seasoning of salt and plenty of pepper. When cooked, rub through a sieve, and add the *vermicelli*. Cook this in the soup, and serve with slices of toast. Serves 4.

WATERCRESS SOUP

We do not think in this country of cooking watercress, though indeed it can be made into an admirable *purée* in the same way as spinach. One of its most delicious appearances is in Watercress Soup, which is simply made and thickened with potato. The main thing here is to make sure that water only is used for the moistening. Many journalists now writing about this soup invariably recommend the use of stock (or the omnipresent chicken *bouillon* cube) for this purpose. To get the fullest flavour of the cress and potato nothing but water should be used. One trial will undoubtedly convince.

1 bunch watercress (small)	2 cups milk
2 oz butter	salt and pepper
¾ pint water	1 egg-yolk
2 potatoes (medium to large)	1 tablespoon milk (or cream)

Pick off the leaves from the watercress, and wash them well. Put them into a saucepan with a good piece of butter (the size of a small egg) and let them melt slowly. Now add hot water, and the potatoes, peeled and cut in thin slices. Put on the lid, and boil quickly for half an hour. Rub the whole through a sieve, put the *purée* back on the heat, and add the boiled milk. Bring to the boil for a moment, season it, and the soup is ready. Bind with an egg-yolk beaten in the milk or cream. Serves 4.

EGGS

EGGS A LA DREUX

These pretty little poached castles flecked with pink and green make
a delicious savoury or breakfast dish.

6 eggs
4 oz lean cooked ham (or bacon)
1 dessertspoon parsley
½ gill cream

1 oz butter
salt and pepper
cayenne
toast

Butter well half a dozen patty-pans each large enough to hold one egg,
mix the ham, finely chopped, with the parsley, and sprinkle the inside
of the pans with this mixture so that each is well lined with it. Now
break an egg carefully into each, season with salt, pepper and a touch
of cayenne, and put a sixth of the cream on top. Dot each with a tiny
piece of butter. Poach them in a pan of boiling water in the oven, and,
when the whites are set, turn them out on to rounds of buttered toast.
Serves 6.

EGGS MAGDA

These scrambled eggs have a most intriguing taste of herbs and cheese.

6 eggs (scrambled)   1 tablespoon freshly chopped or
2 teaspoons French mustard   1 teaspoon dried mixed herbs
2 oz grated cheese   fried bread

Mix scrambled egg with a little French mustard, grated cheese and
mixed herbs. Garnish with triangular snippets of fried bread. Serves 4.

EGGS MALTAISE

A variation on the theme of the now well-known *Pipérade*, the fresh
flavour of the tomatoes contrasting with the deeper tones of the onion
and the overtone of the curry powder.

½ lb tomatoes   1 teaspoon curry powder
½ lb onions   4 eggs
bacon fat   fried bread (or toast)
salt and pepper

Peel and cut up in small pieces equal quantities of tomatoes and onions,
and fry these slowly in a little bacon fat until you have a soft thick
purée. Season to taste. Now for each half-pound of the mixed vegetables
add a teaspoonful of curry powder (you do not want it to taste too
strongly of curry) and just a little more fat. Cook on for another
quarter of an hour, then stir in with a fork a whole egg for each person.
Cook on, stirring and beating, until the eggs are cooked enough to give
you a smooth, savoury mixture in which all trace of egg has disappeared.
Serve at once, garnished with triangles of toast or fried bread. Serves 4.

EGGS POLONAISE

Paul Reboux's interesting theory of *Le Croquant* (the contrast of smooth
and crisp in a single dish) is illustrated here with the help of scrambled
egg and fried bread *croûtons*. The subtle oniony flavour of the chives
lends added interest.

4–5 eggs   salt and pepper
1 tablespoon cream   1 teacup stale bread
1 teaspoon parsley   3 tablespoons butter
1 teaspoon chives

Beat four or five eggs with the cream and add the finely chopped parsley and chives, a good seasoning of salt and pepper and tiny dices of stale bread previously very crisply fried. Scramble this mixture with two tablespoonfuls of butter until it is thick enough to spread, and then fry spoonfuls of it on each side in the remaining butter until golden. Serves 4.

FROMAGE D'ŒUFS

Egg Mayonnaise is a favourite *hors d'œuvre* with nearly everyone, especially if anchovies accompany it. Here is an unusual and rather exciting way of presenting them. The mayonnaise may be tinted pink with tomato paste or lobster coral, or green with a *purée* of parsley, watercress and spinach, or more elaborately with the ingredients used to colour and flavour Montpelier Butter.

8 eggs	chives
butter	chervil
mayonnaise	tarragon
parsley	

Break the eggs into a buttered low *soufflé* dish of a size just large enough to hold them rather crowdedly, and see that they are broken carefully, so that the yolks are intact. Then place the dish in the oven in a baking-tin of boiling water, and cook for ten minutes. When cold, the cake of eggs should be turned out on to a dish, and coated with mayonnaise sauce flavoured with chopped *fines herbes*, that is parsley, chives, chervil, and tarragon. Serves 4.

OMELETTE BOULOGNAISE

The extreme fishiness of soft herring roes is anathema to some who will nevertheless find them more acceptable when encased in egg. This omelette is one way of doing it, another being to egg-and-breadcrumb the roes and fry them in shallow butter or deep oil. Another and more expensive way of serving them will be found on page 34.

12 oz soft herring roes	*maître d'hôtel* butter
1 omelette	

Poach the soft herring roes and use them to stuff a plain omelette, mixing them with a little *maître d'hôtel* butter. When the omelette is stuffed and dished, pour a little of the same butter melted round it. Serves 6.

SCRAMBLED EGGS (NEW YORK STYLE)

A combination of scrambled egg, ham or bacon, onions and mushrooms makes a change from the more usual luncheon or supper dish.

1 slice uncooked ham (or gammon or bacon)	2 tablespoons onion
water	4–5 mushrooms (small)
1½ tablespoons butter	6 eggs (scrambled)
	parsley

Have ready a thin slice of uncooked ham or gammon or bacon, and soak it in lukewarm water for half an hour. Then cut it up in narrow strips; there should be about a breakfastcupful. Melt the butter in a frying-pan and fry in it the chopped onion and strips of bacon. After five minutes, add four or five smallish mushrooms, peeled and sliced, and cook for another five minutes together. Mix well and use as a border to surround ordinary scrambled egg. Sprinkle over all a little chopped parsley. Serves 4.

FISH

ANGELS ON HORSEBACK

In the English *gourmet's* eyes the finest savoury in the world, the inimitable flavour of the oyster contrasting perfectly with the crisply grilled sliver of smoked bacon surrounding it.

oysters	toast
bacon	butter

Wrap each raw oyster in a thin rasher of bacon, and impale them on little skewers. Grill them if you can, otherwise bake them in a hot oven, and when the bacon is crisp arrange them on pieces of buttered toast.

BRILL AUX COURGETTES

The little vegetable marrows known in Italy and France as *courgettes* are delicious as a vegetable dish by themselves, as is shown on page 72.

The companionship of an attractive fish like brill emphasizes their appeal to the diner.

1½–2 lb filleted brill or 2–2½ lb brill	1 pinch basil
2 oz butter	salt and pepper
8 *courgettes*	lemon juice
4 tomatoes	1 tablespoon breadcrumbs

Fillet the fish and arrange it in a shallow fireproof dish which you have buttered beforehand. Now peel the little marrows (they should be four or five inches long) and cut them in long slices, arrange them over the fish with some peeled and coarsely chopped tomatoes and a pinch of chopped basil. Add salt and fresh black pepper. Now sprinkle over a little lemon juice and then some melted butter, put a buttered paper over the top, and cook in the oven until the fillets are done. Then sprinkle with breadcrumbs and more butter, and brown quickly. Serves 4.

COD WITH HORSERADISH

An accompaniment of parsley or egg sauce is generally the fate of the wrongly despised boiled cod, but added interest is lent by the use of horseradish. The conventional onion or leek sauce will have much the same effect on the surprised guest, who will no doubt be delighted with the new experience.

2 lb cod (or hake)	salt and pepper
1 pint fish stock (or water)	1 tablespoon lemon juice
2 tablespoons butter	2 tablespoons horseradish
2 tablespoons flour	

Cook the cod or hake, sliced or whole, in fish stock or water and, when it is done, drain it and keep it warm. With the butter, the flour and sufficient of the fish stock make a thick sauce. Flavour this with salt, pepper and lemon juice, and finally add the grated horseradish. Do not cook after the horseradish has been added, and pour it all over the fish on serving. Serves 4.

COLD MACKEREL

This gamy fish is not often served cold as an *hors d'œuvre*, but Madame Prunier taught us to like it when she opened her restaurant in the late 1930s. The most satisfactory way of preserving its flavour is to grill instead of boiling it; the addition of a pinch (no more) of fresh fennel to the sauce is a great improvement.

4 mackerel	4 peppercorns
court-bouillon:	1 blade mace
2 pints water	1 tablespoon wine vinegar
parsley stalks	½ pint mayonnaise sauce
1 carrot	fennel ⎫
½ onion	parsley ⎭ or *fines herbes*
1 bayleaf	

Either split them, behead and betail them, and poach them in a *court-bouillon* with vinegar, or score them on each side and grill them. But in either case let them get cold, skin them, and serve them covered with mayonnaise sauce to which, if you like, you can add some *fines herbes* or, better still, just a little chopped parsley and fennel. Serves 4.

CREOLE FISHCAKES

The herbs and garlic make all the difference between a Littlehampton boarding-house in the 1890s and the more colourful Caribbean.

1 lb white fish (cooked)	1 tablespoon butter
1 onion	6 tablespoons breadcrumbs
parsley	salt and pepper
thyme	1 egg
1 clove garlic	cooking fat (or butter) for frying

Flake up the remains of any white cooked fish with a finely chopped onion, parsley, thyme, and a touch of garlic. Mix well together, adding a tablespoonful of the butter and one-third of the volume of the mixture in breadcrumbs. Season. Shape into cakes or balls, roll them in beaten egg and then in breadcrumbs, and fry in butter or deep fat until golden. Serves 4.

CURRIED PRAWNS

This simple and authentic Indian Curry Sauce is admirable for doing up any sort of cooked fish, meat or eggs. The inclusion of the garlic is most important to my mind, as it seems to act as the perfect foil to the spiciness of the curry powder.

2 onions (small)	½ lb tomatoes
2 oz butter	¾ pint water
½–1 clove garlic	1 lb prawns
1 tablespoon curry powder	rice
salt	

Fry the onions, finely sliced, in the butter, add (if you will take my advice) a clove or half a clove of garlic. Stir in the curry powder, and season with salt. Now add the peeled and quartered tomatoes, and a little water, enough to make a thickish sauce. Simmer this for a little, then put in the prawns, fresh or from a tin or glass, and let them cook very gently indeed for a quarter of an hour. Serve with very dry and hot plain boiled rice. Serves 4.

EEL MATELOTE

When I was a young man my wife and I used to travel on a bus from Highgate to Hampton Court for the special purpose of dining at the Mitre Hotel there. It was in those days celebrated for its lobster cutlets (see page 36), roast duckling and green peas and deliciously small apple pies each baked in a dish just large enough for one. But what I came to enjoy more than anything was the fried eels and the more elaborate *Matelote* for which a recipe follows:

2 lb eels	1 clove garlic
4 oz minced onion	1 sherry-glass brandy
parsley	¾ oz flour
thyme	¾ oz butter
bayleaf	12 button onions
salt and pepper	¼ lb mushrooms
1 bottle red wine	6 *croûtons*

Cut the prepared eels into pieces about two or three inches long. Now, in a shallow saucepan or frying-pan (a real French *sauté*-pan is the best), put your pieces of eel, the minced onion, a bouquet of parsley, thyme and bayleaf, a good pinch of salt, and the red wine. If you take my advice you will also add a small piece of garlic, crushed, the size of a haricot bean. Bring quickly to the boil, pour in the brandy, and set it alight. When it has burned out, put on the lid, and boil fairly quickly for a quarter of an hour. Then take the pieces of eel out and keep them warm. Strain the liquor into a basin, rinse the pan in hot water, and pour the liquor back again. Continue to boil it until you have reduced it by a third, then add the flour kneaded with two small 'nuts' of butter, and boil for two minutes. Add pepper and a few button onions and mushrooms which you have previously cooked in butter. Put in the pieces of eel, and simmer all together for five minutes. Arrange the pieces of fish on your dish, surround them with the onions and the mushrooms, pour over the sauce (which you have finished with a few bits of butter), and finally set round half a dozen *croûtons* of fried bread. Serves 6.

EELS, JELLIED

I used to be able to buy this plebeian delicacy at a shop in the forecourt of London Bridge Station, for a private eel-gorge in the depths of Surrey. They are good enough, but not a patch on the recipe for the more sophisticated version which can be found on page 28.

2 lb eels	6 peppercorns
2 onions (large)	1½ pints water
2 carrots (medium)	

Cut the skinned eels into two-inch lengths, and put them into a saucepan on a bed of vegetables consisting of the onions and carrots, both sliced, and a few peppercorns. Just cover with cold water, bring slowly to the boil, then cover the pan and simmer gently for an hour or so, until the pieces are quite tender. Then take them out with a perforated spoon and put them into a deep dish; reduce the cooking liquid by rapid boiling by about a third, then strain it over the eel. Leave in a cool place where the jelly will set. Serves 6.

ESCABECHE

This curiously named 'souse' is, I think, of Spanish origin, and I have wondered whether it is related to the Scots 'caveach'. A version of the name appears again as 's'kveitch'.

4 red mullet (or herring, smelts, fillets of sole)	¼ pint wine vinegar
	¼ wineglass water
flour	2 chilli peppers
oil	1 sprig thyme
⅙ finely minced carrot (medium)	1 bayleaf
1 finely minced onion (medium)	salt
3 cloves garlic	

It is particularly good for small red mullet, but other fish like small herrings, smelts, or fillets of white fish like sole can be treated in the same way. Flour the fish and plunge them into smoking hot oil, leaving them there for an instant or two only. Take them out and arrange them in a shallow dish. Leave the oil on one side. In a little pan sweat the finely minced onion, carrot and garlic for ten minutes. Add the remainder of the oil, the wine vinegar, water, chilli peppers, thyme and bayleaf with a little salt and, after heating it gently for ten to fifteen minutes, pour it over the fish. After they have lain in this for twenty-four hours, serve them as they are. Serves 4.

FILETS DE SOLES MURAT

This particularly attractive mixture of fish, potatoes and artichoke *fonds* is inclined to suffer from the unscrupulous chef, who may substitute vegetable marrow for the artichoke bottoms. One such did so to my knowledge at a leading Brighton hotel.

2 soles	1 lb potatoes
¼ pint milk	4 artichoke bottoms
2 oz flour	lemon juice
3 oz butter	parsley

Have the fish filleted, and cut each fillet diagonally into small strips about half an inch wide. Dip these in milk, then in flour, and fry them golden in a little butter. Meanwhile have ready some little cubes of fried potatoes and some cubes of artichoke bottoms which have been tossed in butter. Mix these with the pieces of sole, and pour over them some lightly browned butter flavoured with lemon juice. At the last moment sprinkle over some finely chopped parsley. Serves 4.

FISH BALLS

Though these can well be made with fresh fish, the authentic American recipe calls for salt cod. This at one time only made its appearance on the orthodox Christian table once a year, on Good Friday, but it is now so easy to obtain dried salt cod all through the year from continental delicatessen shops that the ingredient originally specified can be used.

Another very pleasant dish with salt cod and eggs will be found on page 39.

1 breakfastcup salt cod	pepper
2 breakfastcups potatoes	1 egg
water	cooking fat
½ tablespoon butter	

Soak the salt cod, and cut into small pieces. Peel and cut up some potatoes in even-sized pieces. Now cook the fish and the potatoes together in boiling water and, when the potatoes are nearly soft, drain thoroughly. Put back into the pan, and dry them over the heat, then mash up well (without lumps!), add the butter, a good seasoning of pepper, and the well-beaten egg. Beat all this up together for two minutes, then take in spoonfuls and drop into deep fat. Serves 4.

A FISH PIE

1 lb cod	3 oz grated cheese
1 lb potatoes	2 tablespoons breadcrumbs
¾ pint white sauce	

Boil and divide into large flakes some cod, and parboil about the same amount of potatoes. Cut these in slices, and in a rather deep fireproof dish put layers of potato, cod, white sauce and grated cheese until the dish is full. Let the last two layers be potato and the sauce. Now sprinkle it well with grated cheese and breadcrumbs, and cook in the oven until the top is nicely browned. Serves 4.

FRIED SCALLOPS

To many the faint fishy flavour of scallops is quite irresistible, and this is brought out to its fullest when they are simply fried in butter. They should then be served with an *Hollandaise* or a *Béarnaise* sauce. The French name for them is *Coquilles Saint Jacques*, and there is a whole legend concerning them and St James of Compostella.

6–8 scallops	1 oz butter (or cooking fat)
1 egg	olive oil (optional)
2 tablespoons breadcrumbs	lemon juice (optional)

The white part is simply cut in rounds about the size of a very large half-crown, then egg-and-breadcrumbed, and fried golden in clarified butter for about eight minutes. I am told they may be fried in deep fat, too, but I think the slightly slower cooking in butter would be preferable. Some cooks like to soak them first in a little olive oil and lemon juice for half an hour, but if they are fresh and young there is no need for this extra trouble. Serve with Sauce *Hollandaise*. Serves 4.

HALIBUT WITH GREEN PEPPERS

Sweet green peppers are unusual with fish in this country, and this is a notable exception. They give the halibut a very pleasant peppery flavour.

1½ lb halibut	2 tomatoes (large)
1 oz butter	1 sweet green pepper (large)
salt and pepper	½ pint fish stock

Butter a fireproof dish and lay in it the halibut steak, sprinkling it with salt and pepper. On top arrange slices of tomato and some very thin strips of green sweet pepper. Pour in stock and bake in a hot oven, basting frequently, for half an hour. Serves 4.

HERRINGS

Herrings are not the common stuff they used to be. They are even known to be fashionable and come under the category of the fishes that impelled one of Madame Prunier's customers at her London restaurant to say to her, 'Oh, Madame Prunier, you give us fishes which we wouldn't dream of eating anywhere else; you call them by a funny French name, and we adore them.' Here are four recipes of discovery.

Herrings à la Diable

4 herrings	1 tablespoon parsley
1 dessertspoon French mustard	1 tablespoon chervil
4 tablespoons breadcrumbs	1 tablespoon tarragon
olive oil	1 shallot
Sauce Ravigote:	2 pinches salt and pepper
1 tablespoon vinegar	3–4 tablespoons olive oil
1 teaspoon capers	

Score the herrings on each side in three or four places, and spread them with a little made mustard (French mustard being the best, as English may be a bit too hot). Sprinkle them with browned breadcrumbs, and grill them, basting them with olive oil as they cook. Hand with them a *Sauce Ravigote*, which is a mixture of oil, vinegar, capers, parsley, chervil, tarragon and onions all finely chopped, and a seasoning of salt and pepper. (This is the cold one; the hot *Ravigote* being a fish *velouté* flavoured with a reduction of half white wine and half vinegar, finished with shallot butter, and completed by a chopping of chervil, chives and tarragon.) Serves 4.

Herrings à la Portière

4 herrings	1 oz butter
½ gill milk	1 dessertspoon mustard
salt and pepper	1 dessertspoon parsley
1 tablespoon flour	1 teaspoon vinegar

Score the herrings once or twice on each side, and dip them in a little milk. Season them with salt and pepper, and roll them in flour. Heat a little butter in a frying-pan, and put in the herrings, frying them on both sides until they are evenly cooked. Now arrange them on a dish, brush them over with mustard, not too stiff, and sprinkle them with chopped parsley. Put some more butter in the pan in which the fish were cooked, and cook it until it colours a little and smells nutty. Pour it quickly over the herrings, pour a dash of vinegar into the pan, and pour this over the fish, too. Serves 4.

2

Herrings Calaisienne

4 herrings	8 mushrooms (large)
4 soft herring roes	2 oz *maître d'hôtel* butter
2 shallots	½ oz butter
1 dessertspoon parsley	

Split the herrings open, bone them, and stuff them with their own soft roes, chopped shallots, parsley, and mushrooms mixed with *maître d'hôtel* butter. Wrap each up in buttered paper, twist the ends securely so as to make the little bags as airtight as possible, and bake them in the oven for about twenty minutes to half an hour. Serve them in the bags. Serves 4.

Herrings Nantaise

4 herrings	2–3 oz butter
1 tablespoon flour	4 soft herring roes
1 egg	1 teaspoon made mustard
2 tablespoons breadcrumbs	1 *bouquet garni*

Score the herrings in three or four places on each side, flour and egg-and-breadcrumb them. Cook them in a little butter until golden on each side, and serve them with a sauce made from their mashed soft roes, cooked as follows: cook them gently in an ounce of butter, a little water and a *bouquet garni*, put through a strainer, mouli or tammycloth, flavour with the mustard and finish with butter. Serves 4.

HERRING ROES DE LUXE

Soft herring roes on toast were a favourite savoury in Victorian times, a bit middle-class, but not if they were prepared and served as described below.

4 herring roes	1 teaspoon mustard
1 glass white wine (dry)	4 slices toast
2 oz butter	1 dessertspoon parsley
salt and pepper	1 dessertspoon chives

Cook some soft herring roes in a little dry white wine with a pat of butter, and when they are done, drain them, and season them with salt and pepper. Mix some mustard with butter and spread rounds of toast with it. Put a roe on each and sprinkle with chopped parsley and chives. Serves 4.

HOLLENDEN HALIBUT

6 thin slices blanched pickled pork
1 onion (medium)
1 bayleaf
2 lb halibut

4 tablespoons butter
3 tablespoons flour
1 tablespoon breadcrumbs
¾ pint white sauce

One of the really good and simple American dishes. Put the slices
of blanched pickled pork in a fireproof dish, spread some thinly sliced
onion over them, and add a piece of bayleaf. On this bed lay the halibut
and spread over it three full tablespoonfuls of butter kneaded with an
equal quantity of flour. Sprinkle with buttered breadcrumbs, and
arrange a few narrow strips of the pork on top. Cover with buttered
paper, and bake for thirty-five minutes in a moderate oven. Then take
off the paper, and bake for another quarter of an hour. Serve with
white sauce. Serves 6.

HOT CRAB

Crab is usually dressed cold but the hot version does a great deal to
bring out the true flavour of this crustacean. The flesh can also be
dignified by being bound with a light cheese sauce and used to fill little
pastry turnovers, which are then baked in the oven and served hot.
MOCK CRAB SALAD (see next recipe) is as its name betrays not crab
at all but an ingenious fake salad which many will find useful in an
emergency.

1 crab
6 oz water biscuits (or cream
    crackers)
1 tablespoon mushroom ketchup
4 egg-yolks (hard-boiled)
salt and pepper

cayenne
1 egg
1 tablespoon breadcrumbs
    (optional)
1 oz butter

Put a layer of the soft part of the crab in the bottom of the cleaned
shell, then cover this with a layer of pounded water biscuits or cream
crackers. On this arrange the fleshy part of the claws, pouring over
the mushroom ketchup. Sprinkle over some hard-boiled yolks of egg
roughly chopped, season with salt, black pepper, and a little cayenne,
smooth over this the rest of the soft part of the crab, brush with beaten

egg, and sprinkle liberally with more biscuit or breadcrumbs. Dot with
a few pieces of butter, and bake it in the oven for twenty minutes to
half an hour. Serves 4.

Mock Crab Salad

1½ lb cod   2 tablespoons made mustard
paprika pepper   1 tablespoon olive oil
cayenne   4 tablespoons Cheddar (or
salt   *Gruyère*)
¼ pint anchovy vinegar

Tear cooked cod flakes into shreds with two forks (it should look
rather like crab flesh when done), put them into a bowl and season
with paprika pepper, a suspicion of cayenne and a little salt, and moisten
it with a dressing made from the anchovy vinegar, mustard and olive oil.
Sprinkle over the top of this finely grated dry cheese (Cheddar or
Gruyère, but not *Parmesan*) and mix the whole thing lightly together.
Keep it cold until wanted. Serves 4.

LOBSTER NEWBURG

After *à l'Américaine*, this is the best and richest of lobster dishes. Most
amateur cooks are deterred by the idea of cutting up a live lobster, but
the version below compromises with a cooked one.

1 lobster   4 egg-yolks
1 oz butter   1½ gills cream
3 fluid oz sweet sherry (or
   Madeira)

Cut the lobster in pieces, and put them with the butter in a pan large
enough to hold them all on the bottom. Fry them for five or six minutes,
turning them over once (the reddish skin of the lobster will impart a
rosy tint to the butter and eventually to the sauce), then add enough
sweetish sherry or Madeira nearly to cover them, put on the lid, and
cook quickly so that in about fifteen minutes the wine will have reduced
to about three spoonfuls. Now pour in the mixture of yolks of egg and
cream, and shake this gently (do not stir it) over the heat until it
gradually thickens and gets like a pinkish custard. Serves 2.

QUICHE DE SAUMON FUME

A remarkable smoked salmon tart, for a light luncheon or supper dish.
If wanted for a very light first course, the pastry case can be omitted
and the fish custard baked in little *dariole* moulds. By the way, it is not
a success if eaten cold, as the fish tends to toughen.

¾ lb short-crust pastry	grated nutmeg
4 eggs	butter
2 egg-yolks	¼–½ lb smoked salmon (very thinly
¾ pint cream	sliced)
salt and pepper	

Line an 8″ flan case with short-crust pastry. Beat up lightly, as if for an
omelette, the eggs and yolks, mix with them the fresh cream, season
with salt, pepper and grated nutmeg, and pour this mixture into the
flan case. Sprinkle over the top some small dabs of butter, and add
enough thin slices of smoked salmon to cover the cream. Bake in a very
hot oven for thirty-five minutes. Serve immediately, or the salmon will
get tough. The slices should remain on top of the flan and be lightly
covered with cream. Serves 4.

RED MULLET

This fish, sometimes called the Woodcock of the Sea for the reason
that it is generally cooked undrawn, is a distinctly acquired taste. This
is because the cook, I think, has misinterpreted the instructions and left
the whole of the insides in the fish instead of only the liver. If this
proper course is followed, it will make all the difference to the gamy
flavour. Here are three recipes to try.

Red Mullet Montesquieu

4 red mullet	2 tablespoons chives
salt and pepper	1 tablespoon parsley
2 oz butter	1 lemon (juice only)

Have the fillets seasoned with salt and pepper and rolled in melted
butter into which you have chopped some chives and parsley. Then
fry them in a little butter, and serve them with nut-brown butter
(*beurre noisette*) seasoned with lemon juice and chopped parsley.
Serves 4.

Red Mullet Livournaise

4 red mullet	½ wineglass white wine (dry)
3 tomatoes	2 tablespoons breadcrumbs
1 tablespoon oil	1 oz butter (optional)
2 shallots	lemon juice
½ clove garlic	1 teaspoon capers
salt and pepper	

Score and season the red mullet on both sides, arrange them in a fireproof dish, and cover them with chopped tomatoes which have been lightly stewed in oil with chopped shallot, a tiny bit of crushed garlic and salt and pepper. Add a little dry white wine, sprinkle with browned breadcrumbs and melted butter or oil, and bake in a moderate oven for fifteen to twenty minutes, according to the size of the fish. When serving, sprinkle them with a few drops of lemon juice and scatter over a few capers. Serves 4.

Red Mullet Niçoise

4 red mullet	1 clove garlic (small)
olive oil	6 black olives
salt and pepper	½ glass white wine (dry)
4 tomatoes	1 tablespoon parsley
1 onion (medium)	

Brown the mullet on both sides in a little olive oil, season them with salt and pepper, and arrange them in a shallow fireproof dish. Surround them with roughly chopped tomatoes, a little minced onion, the garlic (also chopped), and stoned black olives. Pour over all the wine, and bake in a moderate oven with the lid on until tender. Serve in the same dish cold, sprinkled with chopped parsley. Serves 4.

SALMON TAIL

The simplest way, especially with a prime fish like salmon, is often by far the best, as I think this recipe will prove. If you think the sauce is too plain, I suggest a Mayonnaise or *Hollandaise*, either of which could be garnished with chopped chives or tiny cubes of raw cucumber.

3 lb salmon	butter (for grilling)
½ gill olive oil	2 tablespoons butter
1 teaspoon thyme (chopped)	1 teaspoon chervil
2 teaspoons parsley (chopped)	1 teaspoon chives
1 bayleaf	2 teaspoons lemon juice

Let the salmon tail lie for three or four hours in the olive oil, chopped thyme, chopped parsley, and bayleaf. Turn it three times during this marinading. When the time is up, wipe the piece well, and grill it, basting it with butter. When it is cooked on both sides, serve it with a sauce made of the melted butter mixed with the chervil and chives, both chopped, and the lemon juice. Serves 6.

SALT COD WITH EGGS

1½–2 lb salt cod	pepper
3–4 oz butter	½ lemon (juice only)
6 eggs	*croûtons* (optional)

Soak and boil the cod, flake it up, drain the flakes as well as possible, and keep them hot. Now melt a good piece of butter in a frying-pan, add the beaten eggs, and cook slowly as for scrambled eggs. While the eggs are solidifying, add the pieces of fish, some more butter, plenty of freshly ground black pepper, and the lemon juice. Finish cooking all together, and serve as it is, very hot, with perhaps some triangular *croûtons* of fried bread. Serves 4.

SCALLOPS EN COQUILLE

When I was a lad, scallops were accounted invalid fare, and it was not until my mother gave me Marcel Boulestin's first little book that I discovered an enchanting savoury dish with them. Here it is, and it is a real revelation.

6–8 scallops	3–4 mushrooms
water	2 oz butter
1 tomato	¼ pint *Béchamel* (or white sauce)
1 onion (small)	cream (or breadcrumbs)
1 dessertspoon parsley	

Put the scallops in cold water, bring to the boil, and poach them for five minutes. Take them out, drain them, and cut them up small. Mix them with the flesh of a skinned tomato in little bits, a very small onion, some parsley, and three or four mushrooms finely chopped together. Cook these all together in butter for a few minutes, season them, and then bind them with a little thick *Béchamel* or white sauce. Put this mixture into the shells, and after sprinkling them either with a little cream or with fine breadcrumbs, brown them in the oven.

SMOKED SALMON TOASTS

4 soft herring roes	chervil
salt	4 thin slices smoked salmon
cayenne	1 oz butter
1 dessertspoon parsley	4 pieces toast (buttered)
chives	

Sprinkle some soft herring roes with salt, cayenne and finely chopped parsley, chives and chervil. Wrap each in a very thin slice of smoked salmon, and cook them very gently in butter until the roes are done. Set them then on pieces of hot buttered toast, and serve. Serves 4.

SOLE AU VIN BLANC

This is always turning up in restaurants, but how difficult it is to find a recipe in cookery books. (While writing of sole, let me add a simple dish that wants a lot of beating, with spinach.)

1 onion	1 oz butter
2 sole (large, or 4 small)	1 oz flour
salt	2 egg-yolks
¾ glass white wine (dry)	cream

Butter a fireproof dish, and arrange in it four or five thin rounds of onion. Put on this bed your lightly salted sole, skinned side downwards. Add the wine, bring to the boil on the top of the stove, remove to the oven, and keep the liquid just on the move for about ten minutes, having put a piece of buttered paper over the dish. Meanwhile make a *roux* with butter and flour, moisten it with the strained cooking liquor from the sole, bind – off the heat – with the egg-yolks beaten in a little cream, and finish with a piece of butter in small bits. Disembarrass the sole of the onion rings, dish it up, and pour the sauce over it. Brown it very quickly and lightly under the grill. Serves 4.

Sole with Spinach

2 soles
2 tablespoons flour
salt and pepper
4 tablespoons butter

2–3 lb spinach
1 onion (medium)
2 dessertspoons breadcrumbs

Have the fish filleted, flour and season the fillets, and cook them in
butter until golden on each side. Arrange them round a heap of cooked
spinach with which you have mixed some finely minced onion fried
separately in butter. Sprinkle some breadcrumbs over the dish, add
a little melted butter, and brown quickly in the oven. Serves 4.

TIMBALE OF FISH

A grand sort of fish pie well worth the extra trouble it takes to make.
As will be seen it can respond to a number of interesting and even
exciting variations.

1½ lb potatoes
salt and pepper
grated nutmeg
2 eggs
2 oz breadcrumbs
For the sauce:
  1 oz butter

1 oz flour
¼ pint milk
curry powder
anchovy essence
fish leftovers (or tinned crab or
  lobster)
tinned mushrooms (optional)

Cook the potatoes and mash them well. Season them with salt, pepper,
and a little grated nutmeg, and beat into them the egg-yolks. Now
butter a timbale mould, or a *soufflé*-dish plentifully, and sprinkle the
inside all over with breadcrumbs, white or browned. The dish should
be just large enough to hold the potato mixture. Now bake it in the
oven for forty minutes, take it out, cut the top off smartly in one piece,
and scoop out the potato inside to leave a wall all round the sides about
an inch thick. Paint the inside with white of egg, and put the thing
back, lid and all, in the oven to dry. Meanwhile make a sauce with
butter, the flour, and enough milk to give it rather a stiff consistency;
season it with salt, pepper, a spot of curry powder, and a good touch
of anchovy essence. Now, in this sauce, warm up any left-over white fish
you may have, or open a tin of crab or lobster, and add, if you need
more substance, a few tinned and quartered mushrooms. Put this into

the timbale, put on the lid again, and press it well down. Now turn the mould upside down on a dish, and after a few seconds it will turn out perfectly well. Serves 4.

TROUT GRENOBLOISE

How tired we are of Trout Amandine, a mixture which completely robs the fish of its attraction. And why must we always have gigantic and almost tasteless fish set before us? Let us retire into our own kitchens with our own finger trout, as they used graphically to be called, and produce them Grenoble fashion.

4 trout	1 dessertspoon parsley
butter (for frying)	12 capers
2 lemons	

Wipe your trout, flour them, and fry them in a little butter until they are browned on each side. Take them out of the pan and keep them warm, while you let the butter get just a little darker (it should be a light brown), then quickly squeeze the juice from 1 lemon into it and add a sprinkling of chopped parsley. Pour this over the fish, and serve them garnished with chopped capers and slices of raw lemon. Serves 4.

MEAT

BAKED LAMB CUTLETS

The English Hot Pot often tends to be a bit greasy, but this method of capturing the same flavour ensures that fattiness is obviated. The beef stock gives an unexpected touch which adds interest to the combination.

fat

2 onions (large)

1 lb potatoes

1 teacup meat stock (beef preferred)

salt and pepper

4 lamb cutlets (or mutton cutlets) or 8 very small best end cutlets

Fry the sliced onions without browning for a few minutes, and put them into a fairly shallow greased fireproof dish with the sliced raw potatoes and a small teacupful of meat stock, preferably beef. Season with salt and pepper, and bake in a moderate oven for about forty minutes. Meanwhile brown some well-trimmed lamb or mutton cutlets on both sides, and at the end of this time bury them in the mixture. Finish cooking until the cutlets are done and the potatoes browned. Serves 4.

BEEF BOURGUIGNONNE

The most famous of French vinous stews, best when simply made
though some like to cook mushrooms with it, which I consider un-
warranted. A Burgundy wine should be used for best results, but there
are many other wines of this type which could be substituted, notably
a Portuguese one called Periquita.

1 oz butter	parsley
1 tablespoon olive oil	thyme
1 handful button onions (or 1	1 bayleaf
sliced onion)	1 wineglass red wine
1–2 thickish rashers streaky bacon	1 wineglass water
1½ lb stewing beef	salt and pepper
1 dessertspoon flour	

In half butter and half olive oil lightly fry the button onions, or some
sliced onion if you cannot get the little ones, and bacon cut in small
cubes. Then add the stewing beef cut in suitable pieces, and toss these
all together until the meat is also lightly browned all over. Sprinkle
in the flour, and cook on for a minute or two until it browns slightly,
stirring well. Now add a bouquet of parsley, thyme, and bayleaf, and
just cover the meat with a mixture of red wine and water, half and half.
Season with a little salt and pepper, bring to the boil, cover and simmer
very gently for about two hours or until the beef is quite tender, shaking
the pan occasionally. Serves 4.

BRAINS AU BEURRE NOIR

Brains, preferably calf's, should be washed under a running cold tap
and soaked for at least two hours till white; they are then skinned and
blanched in boiling water for three or four minutes. Plunge them then
into cold water and when quite cold cook them for twenty minutes
either in water or stock seasoned with onion and bayleaf or in a *court-
bouillon* with vinegar. A peculiarity of brains, which Escoffier notes,
is that they cannot be overcooked, as the longer they take the firmer
they become. Hand some plainly cooked noodles with this dish.

1 lb brains	1 dessertspoon parsley
salt and pepper	a few drops vinegar
2 oz butter	

Cook the brains in the usual way, slice them and season them with salt and pepper. Now cook the butter in a frying-pan until it browns well but does not start to burn. Add a small sprinkling of parsley, without cooking it, and pour this over the brains. Now quickly swill the pan with a few drops of good vinegar, and pour this over as well. Serves 4.

BREAST OF LAMB

For some years in the 'thirties I used to lunch every day in the Waldorf Grill in Aldwych and there I learned to find out from an accommodating waiter or from the chef himself what he (the chef) was having for his own lunch that day. In this way many interesting dishes came to light, among them the following way with lamb which in my opinion is quite superfine for a simple dish.

2 lb breast of lamb	$\frac{1}{4}$ turnip (small)
parsley	salt
thyme	6 peppercorns
bayleaf	2 oz breadcrumbs
1 onion (small)	1 oz butter
6 cloves	brown sauce (or tomato sauce)
2 carrots	egg or flour-and-water batter

First cook the piece of breast in the usual way with a bouquet of parsley, thyme, and bayleaf, a small onion stuck with half a dozen cloves, the sliced carrot, and turnip cut in dice. Add salt and a few peppercorns, and just cover the meat with boiling water. Skim and cook until the bones will slip out; then take them out and press the meat between two plates under a good weight. When it is cold cut it into suitably sized pieces, dip them in egg or flour-and-water batter, coat with fine breadcrumbs, and fry them golden and crisp on each side. Serve well drained with a brown or tomato sauce. (There is a great deal to be said for the French way of eating this dish with mustard and a separate dish of pickled gherkins.) Serves 4.

CALF'S LIVER

Liver makes a highly suitable vehicle, as the stage expression goes, to the *Provençal* sauce and garnish so popular after the advent of garlic to our dishes.

Liver à la Provençale

1½ lb liver	6 tomatoes
salt and pepper	2 liquid oz olive oil
2 tablespoons flour	½ clove garlic
2 tablespoons olive oil	1 pinch sugar
2 teaspoons parsley	

Cut the liver in slices, season them, flour them lightly, and fry them in olive oil. Arrange them on a dish and sprinkle with a little parsley. Serve separately some *Provençal* sauce which you will have made as follows. Peel the ripe tomatoes, remove the pips, and press out the water. Chop up the red flesh that remains and put it into a saucepan in which you have ready smoking the olive oil. Season with salt and pepper, add the garlic, crushed, the sugar, and a teaspoonful of chopped parsley. Cook gently for twenty minutes only, and your sauce is ready. Serves 4.

Calf's Liver, Fried

1½ lb liver	1 tablespoon chopped parsley
salt and pepper	fat
1 onion (small)	lemon

Cut the liver into one-inch cubes, sprinkle these with salt and pepper and cover them with the thinly sliced onion and the parsley. Leave for two hours, remove the onion and parsley, and fry in hot, deep fat for one minute only. Serve garnished with lemon. Serves 4.

CARBONNADE FLAMANDE

The substitution of beer for the red wine of *bœuf bourguignonne* shows what a beer-drinking part of Europe can do with beef, bacon and onions.

2–3 lb beef	1 lb onions
salt and pepper	1 clove garlic
2–3 oz butter	2 lumps sugar
2–3 oz bacon	vinegar
2 tablespoons flour	1½ lb potatoes
¼–½ pint beer	

Cut thin flank of beef, or other cheap cut, into two-inch lengths, season them with salt and pepper, and brown them in the butter. Add the lean bacon, cut in small dice, and brown these too. Take out the meat, pour off all the butter except about two tablespoonfuls, add to this the flour, and cook to a light-brown colour. Then moisten with beer to make a sauce. Fill an earthenware casserole with alternate layers of browned onions, the beef and the bacon dice, adding the garlic, sugar, a seasoning of salt and pepper, and the sauce. Cover and simmer gently for two and a half to three hours, adding more beer if necessary as it cooks. Just before serving add a dash of vinegar, and accompany it by boiled potatoes. Serves 4 to 6.

CERVELLES MONTROUGE

This Brain Tart should be served as a very unusual course for a light luncheon. Notes on the cooking of brains will be found on page 44. My own counsel here is to see that the sauce for the mushrooms is not too heavily flavoured with cheese.

1 8″ pastry flan (already cooked
   this equals ¾ lb shortcrust paste)
2 lb brains
¼ lb mushrooms
¼ pint cream

For the sauce:
½ oz butter
½ oz flour
½ pint milk
1–1½ oz cheese
salt and pepper
1 egg-yolk

Bake a pastry flan, and arrange in it overlapping slices of cold cooked brains. Garnish these with minced cooked mushrooms bound with cream, and cover the whole thing with a light cheese sauce which has been bound with an egg-yolk. Brown quickly, and serve at once. Serves 6.

CHOPS, STUFFED

Interesting enough, but more so if some application has been made in the choice of stuffing. But see that the chops are well trimmed of fat beforehand or disaster lies in wait for you.

4 loin chops
6 oz stuffing—sage and onion or
   forcemeat or sausage meat

2 oz breadcrumbs
1 egg
4 oz butter (or fat)

Leave the bone on some loin chops, and cut through the meat horizontally, so that a deep pocket is made through to the bone. Stuff this with whatever filling you like, mint stuffing, or sage and onion, veal forcemeat or sausage meat, and then press the sides of the chops lightly together again. Now dip the chops in crumbs, then in beaten egg and then in crumbs again, and bake them in a hot oven, basting with butter or other suitable fat and turning them over once during the cooking. Serves 4.

FILLET OF BEEF SOUBISE

The Englishman prefers his fillet grilled and very seldom roasts it but here is rather a grand way of doing the latter. Insistence must be laid on a good paprika pepper. (See page 14.)

2½–3 lb beef fillet	4 oz butter
larding bacon	¼ pint white sauce
8–12 onions (small)	salt
1 lb onions (medium)	1 pinch castor sugar
½ pint white stock	1 teaspoon paprika pepper
1 oz brown sugar	2 tablespoons cream

Lard the fillet, and roast it in the usual manner – ten minutes to the pound 450° F (Reg 8). When it is done, set it on a long dish and garnish it with small onions which have been cooked in white stock and glazed at the last minute by reducing the stock and adding 1 oz butter and 1 oz brown sugar. The sauce to be handed with this joint is a thin *Soubise* flavoured somewhat highly with paprika pepper. For this, stew a pound of blanched onions, finely chopped, in butter until they are tender. Moisten with thick white sauce, and season with salt and a pinch of castor sugar. Now add the paprika pepper, and cook together very gently for half an hour. Rub through a fine sieve or tammycloth, and finish with cream and 1 oz butter in small pieces. Serves 6 to 8.

GAMMON BAKED IN MILK

When we first came to live in Surrey before the war, we used to lunch occasionally at a small hotel on Abinger Common. Here the innkeeper's wife produced a fashion of baking a gammon rasher which she told us was of Canadian origin. It was extremely good.

2 lb gammon rasher	1 teaspoon mustard (level)
water	1 teaspoon Worcestershire Sauce
⅓ breakfastcup breadcrumbs	1 egg-yolk
3 teaspoons brown sugar (level)	milk

Cover the gammon rasher with cold water, bring it to the boil and boil for ten minutes. Dry it and put it into a baking-dish, and spread it with a paste made of the breadcrumbs, brown sugar, mustard, Worcestershire Sauce and egg-yolk. Pour in enough milk to come three-quarters up the rasher, and bake in a moderate oven for forty minutes, adding a little more milk if it boils away too fast. Serves 6.

GOULASH OF BEEF

Those who like the sweetish taste of paprika pepper (please see page 14) will find this warming and filling winter fare. This is how I like it, plain and simple, but some like to add a small muslin bag of caraway seeds during the cooking.

3 lb beefsteak	1 teaspoon paprika pepper or more
¼ lb lard	to taste
½ lb onions	2 cups water
1 teaspoon salt	1 lb potatoes (small)
1 lb tomatoes	

Fry the beefsteak, cut in one-inch-sided cubes, in the lard with the coarsely chopped onions. When the latter are golden, add the salt, peeled and quartered tomatoes, as much paprika pepper as you like but not less than a teaspoonful, and a cupful of water. Cover, and cook in the oven for an hour and a half, then add the smallish potatoes cut in quarters and another cup of water. Cook again, covered, for an hour or so, when the liquid will have practically disappeared. Serves 6 to 8.

Hungarian Goulash of Beef

1½ lb stewing beef
2 oz lard
¼ lb onions
½ teaspoon salt
½ lb tomatoes

1 teaspoon paprika pepper or more
   to taste
2 teacups water
½ lb potatoes (small)

Fry the cubed stewing beef in the lard with the coarsely chopped
onions until the latter are golden. Then add the salt, peeled and
quartered tomatoes, the paprika pepper, and a teacupful of water. Cover
and cook in a moderate oven for an hour and a half or until the beef
is quite tender. Then add the smallish potatoes cut in quarters and
another teacup of water; put on the lid again and bake for a further
hour or so, until the liquid has almost disappeared. Serves 4.

GRILLED TROTTERS

We have already encountered pig's trotters in a split pea soup (page 17),
and here is something more substantial for those who like this gelatinous
extremity. With mashed potatoes and a pot of French mustard it admits
of few rivals.

2 pig's trotters
1 quart water
salt
6 peppercorns
1 teaspoon allspice
2–3 sprigs parsley

2 sprigs thyme
1 bayleaf
2–3 cloves garlic
a little olive oil
4 tablespoons breadcrumbs

Cut the prepared trotters in half lengthwise and wrap up each half
in a piece of cloth, twisting each end well and tying it. Then cook them
for four or five hours in water with salt, peppercorns, allspice, a large
bouquet of parsley, thyme, and bayleaf, as well as two or three cloves
of garlic. When the trotters are done, take them out of the water, let
them cool, and then unwrap them. Roll them in olive oil, and then in
breadcrumbs, and grill them quickly. A quarter of an hour should be
enough for both sides.

LAMB A LA SAINTE-MENEHOULD

We have already had one dish of breast of lamb, and here is another.
It sounds terribly rich, but the breadcrumbs militate against this being
too sickly. Here again is an excuse for eating mustard with it, *aux fines
herbes* being about the best for the purpose.

3–4 rashers fat bacon	2 tablespoons stock
1 breast of lamb	¼ oz butter
2 carrots	salt and pepper
4 onions	3 tablespoons breadcrumbs
2 bayleaves	½ pint clear gravy
1 sprig thyme	

Put two good rashers of fattish bacon in the bottom of a pan or
casserole, and lay on them some breast of lamb. Cover it with dice of
fat bacon, the sliced carrots, chopped onions, and a bouquet of bayleaves
and a little thyme. Moisten with stock, put on the lid with a piece of
buttered paper under it, and cook gently in the oven for three hours.
Then take the breast out, bone it, season it with salt and pepper,
sprinkle it with breadcrumbs, and put it in the hot part of the oven.
When the breadcrumbs are golden, serve it with clear gravy. Serves 4.

LAMB CUTLETS SUEDOISE

Here is a Swedish dish which once tasted is liable to become a firm
favourite. Whoever invented it, the companionship of apple and horseradish was an inspiration.

8 lamb cutlets	a little olive oil
2 onions (medium)	1 oz butter
1 tablespoon chopped parsley	6 tablespoons breadcrumbs
1 sprig thyme	8 large cooking apples
1 bayleaf	½ gill white wine
1 lemon (juice)	1–2 tablespoons horseradish

Put the cutlets first into a deep dish (they should of course be nicely
trimmed) and sprinkle them with minced onion, parsley, thyme and
bayleaf, the juice of a lemon and a few drops of olive oil. Turn them
over in this once or twice during half an hour or so, then dry them and
wipe off any trace of the mixture they soaked in. Brush them over with

melted butter and then cover with fine white breadcrumbs, pressing
them on with the flat of a knife and shaking off any loose ones afterwards.
Grill them gently and carefully, basting them with the chosen fat, and
serve thus. Make a really thick *purée* of apples, using a little white wine
if possible instead of water for stewing the apples. When the *purée* is
ready, stir in the grated horseradish according to your taste, heap it
up in the middle of your dish, and lean the cutlets round it. Serves 4.

MUTTON, APPLE, AND ONION PIE (SQUAB PIE)

2 oz dripping
1 lb apples
1 lb onions
¾ lb peeled potatoes

salt and pepper
¾–1 lb cold cooked mutton
1 cup water

The story goes that two old Devonshire folk invented this pie (originally
made with pigeons) because one liked onions and the other liked apples.
It is surprisingly good. Fry in dripping some peeled, cored, and sliced
or chopped apples, and an equal quantity of onions. Grease a pie-dish
well, and line it first with raw potato cut in very thin slices. Season this
layer with salt and pepper, and fill up with alternate layers of apple,
onions, and small pieces of mutton, seasoning lightly as you go. Pour
in the water, add a dot or two of the same fat used for the frying, cover
with a final layer of sliced potatoes, and bake until the top is nicely
browned.

OX HEART

Hearts, ox's and calf's, are generally stuffed and roasted in this country,
but rather a nice French recipe may well be preferred. The French,
who are more ingenious in their handling of offal, will even make a
similar dish out of lights, to Pussy's great disgust at her deprivation
of this delicacy.

1 ox heart
1 oz bacon fat (or pickled pork
  fat)
1 heaped tablespoon flour
¾–1 pint red wine or stock

1 large bouquet parsley
1 sprig thyme
1 bayleaf
½ lb button onions

Cut the cleaned and prepared ox heart into squares and colour these in bacon fat or pickled pork fat. Then sprinkle them with flour and moisten with a mixture of half red wine and half stock (the stock may be made with the heart's trimmings). Add a large bouquet of parsley, thyme and bayleaf and cook gently with the lid on for an hour and a half. Now is the time to add some button onions which have first been lightly fried in the same kind of fat, put on the lid again and continue cooking for another hour and a half or until the meat is tender. Serves 4.

OXTAIL

For myself I prefer to cook oxtail in the French manner, using a vigorous red wine as the moistening. It is one of those dishes which improve by being heated up, a procedure which also makes the removal of the surface fat easier. But here is a simple version which is notable for the inclusion of cabbage. In addition a garnish of brussels sprouts and triangular snippets of fried bread turns it into a first-class dish.

1 oxtail	10 onions (small)
1 pig's ear	5 oz carrots
2 pig's trotters	5 oz turnips
water	$\frac{1}{2}$ lb chipolata sausages
salt	$1\frac{1}{2}$ lb potatoes
1 cabbage (small)	

Cut up the tail as usual, and put it into a stewpan with a pig's ear and two pig's trotters, each cut into four or five pieces. Cover with cold water, adding a third of an ounce of salt for each quart, bring to the boil, skim well, and cook gently for a couple of hours. Now add the cabbage cut in quarters and previously parboiled, the little onions, and the carrots and turnips which have been cut in the shape of olives. Cook for another two hours, and then serve the tail with the vegetable garnish, the ear cut in thin strips and some grilled chipolata sausages. You will want no more than plain boiled potatoes with it. Serves 4.

PORTFOLIO HASH

This is a choicer version of Shepherd's Pie, and is well worth the little
extra trouble it takes. The three Escoffier bottled sauces can be a god-
send to the cook in a hurry and the sliced instead of mashed potatoes
something of a novelty.

2 onions (large)	Escoffier's *Sauce Robert* (or *Derby*
fat	*Sauce*, or *Sauce Diable*) to taste
6 cooked potatoes	1 tablespoon breadcrumbs
½–¾ lb cold beef	½ oz butter
½ cup stock	

First fry some chopped onion in a pan, put it aside and, in the same
pan, fry slices of cooked potato. Mix these, and cook them together for
a minute, then put a layer in a shallow fireproof dish. On this layer
put another of your cold meat chopped up or minced and bound with a
sauce lightly diluted with stock. The sauce especially recommended is
Escoffier's *Sauce Robert*, but his *Derby Sauce* and *Sauce Diable* would
do very well. Then put another layer of the potatoes, another of meat,
and a final one of the potatoes, sprinkling this with breadcrumbs.
Sprinkle over a little melted butter, and brown quickly in the oven.
Serves 4.

PICCATE AL MARSALA

This fascinating dish comes from Italy, as its name betrays. Provided
that you have the ingredients handy, it can be cooked in literally five
or six minutes. A grand accomplishment for the show-off hostess.

1½ lb veal	6 tablespoons Marsala
salt and pepper	1 tablespoon white stock
lemon juice	½ lb mushrooms
1 oz flour	1 lb mashed potatoes
1½ oz butter	

Cut some very thin slices of veal, about three inches square and
weighing not more than an ounce each. Flatten them, season them with
salt, pepper and lemon juice and roll very lightly in flour. Brown these
quickly on each side in enough butter to cover the bottom of a heavy
frying-pan, then add a teaspoonful of Marsala for each piece of meat,

let it bubble up and then stir in about a tablespoonful of white stock. Lower the heat, and cook on for a few minutes more until the sauce begins to look syrupy. Then serve at once with some grilled mushrooms and a little mashed potato. The whole of the cooking of this delicious dish should not take more than five minutes. Serves 4.

PORK CHOPS WITH GHERKINS

A *bourgeois* dish from one of Marcel Boulestin's early books. The thickening of the sauce with the breadcrumbs is an unusual touch and might be thought too bready, but it is not, and the presence of the gherkins is a good foil to the richness of the meat.

4 pork chops	1 cup veal stock (or water)
1 oz butter (or lard)	1 teaspoon vinegar
1 handful breadcrumbs	8 small gherkins
1 clove garlic	

Have some pork chops cut as thin as possible, and fry them on both sides in butter or lard. When they are nearly done, throw in a handful of white breadcrumbs and, if you like the flavour, a very little very finely chopped garlic. Fry with the chops until the breadcrumbs are browned, when the chops should be done, add then a cup of hot water (or better, of veal stock if you have some by you), and cook together for a few minutes more, so that the gravy thickens. At the last minute, having arranged the chops on a dish, add a drop of vinegar and some chopped gherkins to the gravy, give it a stir, and pour it over the chops. Serves 4.

PORK CROQUETTES

Nothing could be simpler than this, which may sometimes be found in continental cookery books under the name of *Frikadeller*. They are greatly improved if pickled damsons or peaches are eaten with them.

¾ lb pork	grated nutmeg
1½ lb mashed potatoes	1–2 tablespoons parsley
1 egg	2–3 oz flour
salt and pepper	3 oz butter

Get the butcher to mince you, in his sausage-machine, some raw pork, half fat half lean or, at any rate, two-thirds lean and one-third fat. Mix this well with twice its volume of mashed potato, bind with beaten egg, and season with salt, pepper, grated nutmeg, and finely chopped parsley. Shape into round flat cakes, like fishcakes, flour them, and fry them fairly slowly in butter until they are golden and the meat is cooked. Serves 4.

SAUSAGES

The English 'Banger' these days is much of a muchness, so three different kinds of dishes are given here for the sausage-lover to deal with. The English-size one is rather too large to present in these ways and the chipolata too small, so the longer 'Parisian' type is recommended.

Saucisses au Vin Blanc

12 sausages
1 oz fat
1 glass white wine (dry)
1 teaspoon butter

1 teaspoon flour
1 breakfastcup stock
1 egg-yolk

The thinnish sausages called 'Parisian' are best for this dish. Blanch the sausages for a moment in boiling water, prick them lightly, and fry them. Strain off the fat and, for every twelve sausages, pour over them a glass of dry white wine. Let this slowly reduce to half, while in another pan you make a sauce with butter, flour, and stock. Add the wine to this, and at the last minute bind with the egg-yolk. Pour it over the sausages. Serves 4.

Sausages with Cabbage

1 cabbage
1 quart water
1 lb bacon bones
2 sprigs parsley
1 sprig thyme
1 bayleaf

8–12 sausages
1 oz sausage dripping
pepper
grated nutmeg (or 6 juniper berries)
1 cup stock (beef preferred)

Cut a cabbage into fairly small pieces, and half-cook these in water with bacon bones and a bouquet of parsley, thyme, and bayleaf. By the time the cabbage is ready, have some sausages grilled, and put half the cabbage, well drained, chopped up, and mixed with a little of the sausage dripping into a fireproof dish, seasoning well with pepper and grated nutmeg or, better still if you can get them, some crushed dried juniper berries. Lay the sausages on top, cover them with the rest of the cabbage similarly treated, pour over the stock, preferably beef, and bake for half an hour in a moderate oven. Serves 4.

Sausages with Carrots

1 lb carrots	lemon juice
2–3 oz butter	1 oz sausage dripping
12 sausages	1 glass white wine (dry)
1 dessertspoon parsley	1–1½ lb mashed potatoes
2 onions (medium)	

Cook some baby carrots in butter and cut them in slices. Put them into a shallow fireproof dish and on them arrange some grilled thin sausages (the size called 'Parisian' is the best for this dish). Sprinkle these with a little chopped parsley, some chopped fried onions, a drop or two of lemon juice, some of the fat from the sausages, the dry white wine, and cook together in the oven for just a few minutes longer. Serve as it is, with mashed potato. Serves 4.

TERRINE OF PORK

Long before the days when *pâté* became the rage in even small hotels and restaurants we were happily making our own *pâté*, snobbishly called *pâté de campagne*, out of the simplest ingredients and to the delight of our more ambitious friends, so much nicer than the slabs of garlicky potted meat handed out so frequently nowadays, accompanied by so-called toast Melba instead of the still warm thick-thin slices.

½ lb pig's liver	1 large pinch mixed spice
1½ lb pork	1 pinch grated nutmeg (or mace)
½ lb pickled pork	1 teaspoon mixed herbs
onion (small)	1 handful breadcrumbs
1 clove garlic	1 egg
salt and pepper	butter

Cut up in small pieces the pig's liver, lean pork, streaky pickled pork. Pass these at least once through the mincing machine, and put it all into a large basin. Now season it well with the finely chopped onion, a trifle of minced garlic, plenty of black pepper, some salt, a good pinch of mixed spice, a grating of nutmeg or a pinch of mace, and the mixed herbs. Now add a good handful of finely grated fresh bread-crumbs, and mix it all up with the well-beaten egg. If it is too stiff, a little stock can be added, but it should be about the same consistency as a Christmas Pudding when ready. Put this into your well-buttered terrine, put a piece of buttered paper right on top of the meat, put on the lid, and bake in a moderate oven for about an hour. Serves 6.

TIMBALE OF HAM

There are times when the remains of a ham or gammon of bacon defeats the ingenuity of the best of us, but here is an extremely attractive way of dealing with it, reminiscent of the treatment of the fish timbale on page 41. There is no reason why this one should not be served cold, on a picnic for instance.

1 lb flour	1 onion
2 oz butter	$\frac{1}{2}$ pint cream
6 eggs	pepper
1 gill sour cream (thick)	grated nutmeg
butter	$\frac{1}{2}$–$\frac{3}{4}$ pint tomato sauce
$\frac{1}{2}$–$\frac{3}{4}$ lb ham	

Make a paste with the flour, butter, a beaten egg, and the sour cream. Cut this into several pieces, roll them out thin, and use some of it to line the sides and bottom of a cake-tin which has first been buttered. Mince up your ham, lean and fat together, but not too much fat, and mince the onion with it, until altogether you have a soup plate full. Now beat up five eggs with the cream, mix them with the ham and onion, and season with pepper and a little grated nutmeg, adding salt if necessary. Spread a finger-thick layer of this mixture on the pastry on the bottom of the tin, cover this with a thin layer of pastry, then more mixture, more pastry, and so on until you close the tin with the top layer of pastry. An hour in a hot oven will cook it, and it should be served turned out, with a tomato sauce handed separately. Serves 4.

TOURTE LORRAINE

This highly interesting pork and veal pie is a safe bet for luncheon, when it should be served hot and golden from its last brief session in the oven. The marinating of the two meats gives them a special flavour not usually encountered in this country.

½ lb pork	6 peppercorns
½ lb veal	2–3 cloves
1 onion (large)	½ glass white wine (dry)
1 clove garlic	pastry
1 tablespoon chopped parsley	2–3 eggs
1 teaspoon salt	1 cup cream

Cut some raw pork and veal into thin strips, and let them lie for twenty-four hours in a marinade of onion, garlic, parsley, peppercorns, salt, cloves, and wine. Make some of your best pastry and line a dish with it. On this couch lay your drained and wiped strips of pork and veal, having removed all traces of the marinade, and put on the lid of the tart, leaving a hole in the top in which you stick a little funnel made of kitchen paper. Cook the tart for twenty to twenty-five minutes in a hot oven, and then take it out and pour in through the funnel two or three eggs beaten up with cream and slightly salted. Bake again for another ten minutes, and it is ready. Serves 4.

TRIPES A LA MODE DE CAEN

Those familiar with the great steaming casserole containing this king of offal dishes will no doubt be astonished to learn that it can be bought in tins, but as a matter of fact this should cause no surprise as this kind of long-cooking stew, like oxtail and curry, actually benefits by being warmed up.

2 lb tripe	1 sprig tarragon
1 ox foot	2 sticks celery
1 calf's foot	1 clove garlic
2–3 pieces rind of pickled pork	4 cloves
2 carrots	salt
4 onions	cayenne
3–4 sprigs parsley	1 liqueur glass Calvados (or
1 sprig thyme	brandy)
1 bayleaf	cider (dry)

Take the fine double tripe, scrape it and wash it well, and blanch it for half an hour. Drain it, dry it, and cut it into small squares. Cut also into squares the meat of the ox and calf's feet. In the bottom of your large casserole put the rind of pickled pork, the bones from the feet, the carrots, onions cut in small pieces, a bouquet of parsley, thyme and bayleaf, tarragon, celery, the garlic, cloves, salt, a pinch of cayenne, and the pieces of tripe and meat from the feet. Moisten with Calvados (apple brandy), or brandy would do, and enough dry cider to cover the meat. Put on the lid of the pot, and seal it down with a paste of flour and water, so that it is airtight. Put it in a slow oven, and let the tripe cook for eight hours. On serving, the bones, the vegetables, and the bouquet should be withdrawn, and as much grease as possible removed. Serves 6.

VEAL

Veal is so often boiled or roasted that we tend to forget how admirable it is in stews. These two, one from Italy (*Osso Bucco*) and the other from the Caribbean, are masterpieces of regional cookery, and should find a way on to everybody's table.

Osso Bucco

3 lb knuckle of veal	1 glass white wine (dry)
1 onion	water
1 carrot	parsley
1–2 sticks celery (or celery salt)	thyme
salt and pepper	bayleaf
butter	basil (optional)
1 oz flour	lemon peel
½ pint tomato pulp (or tinned tomato *purée* and water)	

Have the knuckle of veal sawn into two-inch lengths. Chop up the onion, carrot, and celery (or use celery salt in seasoning), and brown them in a stewpan in a little butter. Add the pieces of veal, and brown these too. Add an ounce of butter kneaded with the flour, and let this brown with it. Now add the tomato pulp (or some tinned tomato *purée* diluted with water), the wine, and just enough water barely to cover the meat. Complete with a bouquet of parsley, thyme, and bayleaf (and add, if possible, a little basil), bring to the boil, put on the lid, and simmer for about an hour and a half. Strain the sauce on serving, and add to it at the last moment a little strip of lemon peel chopped up very finely with a few sprigs of parsley. Serves 4.

Veal à la Creole

3 lb brisket of veal	6 tomatoes
½ lb bacon	1 tablespoon wine vinegar (white)
4 potatoes (medium)	parsley
2 onions (large)	thyme
2 carrots (medium)	bayleaf
salt and pepper	marjoram
1 tablespoon lard	cayenne pepper
1 clove garlic	1 glass white wine (dry)
1 tablespoon flour	1½ pints water

Cut the brisket of veal into two-inch squares, lean mild bacon and potatoes into cubes, and onions and carrots into slices. Season the meat with salt and pepper and brown it all over in the lard. Then add the other ingredients, with the minced garlic, and brown them too. Lastly mix in the flour, sliced tomatoes, white wine vinegar, some chopped parsley, thyme, bayleaf and marjoram, a little cayenne pepper, a good glass of dry white wine and the water. Bring to the boil, cover closely and let it simmer for about two hours. Serves 6.

Veal with Olives

Not to be confused with Veal Olives, named after their shape and containing no olives at all. But they give the dish a pleasant rather saltier taste than usual.

2 lb veal	enough water to cover the bottom
1 oz pork fat (or bacon fat)	of the pan to the depth of
6–8 onions (small)	½ inch
1 clove garlic	1 handful olives
1 tablespoon tomato *purée*	

Get a nice piece of veal and brown it all over in pork or bacon fat. Take it out, and put in the same dish a few small onions, the crushed garlic, and tomato *purée*. Add a few spoonfuls of water, put back the piece of veal, and let it cook very gently with the lid on for a couple of hours. After an hour and a quarter, add a handful of stoned olives. Add more water if necessary; it may evaporate if the lid is not very tight-fitting. Serves 4.

VEAL KIDNEY A LA LIEGEOISE

Quite the most delicious way of all of dealing with a veal kidney, which all gin addicts will heartily applaud.

1 veal kidney	1 wineglass burned gin (small)
1 oz butter	2 juniper berries
salt and pepper	1 tablespoon veal gravy

Trim a whole veal kidney, leaving only a very slight layer of fat on it. Heat the butter in a small oval casserole, put the seasoned kidney into this and cook it gently for about thirty minutes, taking care to turn it often. One minute before serving add the burned gin, dried juniper berries and good veal gravy. Serve it in the dish in which it was cooked. Serves 2.

POULTRY AND GAME

CHICKEN PIE

Too often is this lovely pie filled with pre-cooked joints of the chicken, usually because the cook shies at the job of cutting it up raw; but this is a case where frozen chicken joints come in useful.

1 chicken (large)	6 oz veal
1½ oz chopped cooked mushrooms	4–6 rashers bacon
butter	2–3 eggs
1½ oz onions	½ pint chicken stock
1 dessertspoon parsley	puff pastry

Cut the chicken up in convenient pieces, set them out on a dish, and sprinkle them with the chopped mushrooms which have first been cooked in butter, the same quantity of finely chopped onions, and a pinch or two of freshly chopped parsley. On the bottom and sides of your pie-dish lay some thin slices of veal, and then arrange the pieces of chicken, seeing that the legs are at the bottom of the dish where they will cook better. Arrange here and there some thin pieces of bacon and two or three hard-boiled eggs cut in halves or quarters. Three-parts

fill the dish with chicken stock, made so that it will form a fine jelly
if you want to eat the pie cold, cover with a layer of puff pastry, and
bake in a moderate oven for an hour and a half. Pour some more stock
in through the slit when it is done. Serves 6.

COQ AU VIN

This famous dish has in varying amateur versions become almost a
commonplace in the British Isles: and no wonder, for with a little care
nothing could be much simpler or more rewarding to cook. The main
precaution to take is to see that in a moment of enthusiasm you do not
open a bottle of your best vintage Burgundy to do so.

1 cockerel	1 bottle Burgundy
1 wineglass brandy	sugar
½ tablespoon vinegar	parsley
salt and pepper	thyme
½ teaspoon spice	bayleaf
3 oz butter	1 clove garlic
4 oz breast of pork	1 oz flour
4 oz bacon	*croûtons*
12 onions (small)	

Kill a fine young cockerel and save its blood, which you must mix
with two small spoonfuls of brandy and half a tablespoonful of vinegar
to prevent it from coagulating. Cut the bird in pieces as for a *fricassée*,
and sprinkle them with salt, pepper, and spice, leaving them for two
or three hours. An hour and a half before dinner-time, fry in butter
in a stewpan large enough to take the bird, some small pieces of breast
of pork, a few small cubes of bacon, and the onions. When these are
done, add the pieces of the cockerel, and fry these golden, too. Pour
away the fat, add a liqueur glassful of brandy, and set it alight. Then
moisten with a bottle of Burgundy, and season with salt, freshly ground
black pepper, a pinch of sugar, a bouquet of parsley, thyme, and bayleaf,
and garlic. Simmer for an hour and ten minutes. Before serving take
out the pieces of the bird, and keep them warm on a dish. Take out
also the bouquet, and bind the sauce with a tablespoonful of butter
kneaded with flour and, very slowly, the cockerel's blood, being sure
to stir all the time and to avoid bringing the sauce to the boil. Pour
this sauce over the pieces of chicken and garnish with *croûtons* of bread
fried in butter. Serves 6.

GUINEA FOWL AUX CHOUX

This somewhat tasteless, albeit very useful semi-game bird often needs a little tenderising, which this process conveniently does.

1 guinea fowl	2–3 cloves
2 oz lard	parsley
1 cabbage	thyme
6 oz pickled pork	bayleaf
1 onion	1½ pints stock

First brown the guinea fowl in lard in a casserole or an oval pan. Take it out, and put into the pan a third of your cabbage, which has been blanched for ten minutes and well dried, and on this the guinea fowl. Cover it with another layer of cabbage. Now add some cubes of blanched pickled pork, an onion stuck with two or three cloves, and a bouquet of parsley, thyme, and bayleaf. Finish with the rest of the cabbage, and pour in some good well-flavoured stock, to come up nearly to cover the cabbage. The best stock to use is that from which the fat has not been removed. Now bring to the boil on top of the stove, cover the pan with greased paper, and put on the lid. Put into a very moderate oven, and simmer for an hour and a half to two hours. Serves 4.

PARTRIDGE

Partridge à la Crême

Accompanied by *pommes parisiennes* and small runner beans this young partridge easily beats all other hot game dishes.

1 partridge	1 cup cream
1½ oz butter	lemon juice
1 onion (small)	

Simply cook the young partridge in an earthenware casserole, after having browned it lightly in butter, with a smallish onion cut in pieces. When it is three-quarters done, pour over the cream into which you have stirred a few drops of lemon juice. Baste with this while the cooking finishes, and after you have taken out the bird, stir and scrape the bottom of the pan well so that the juices from the bird are well mixed with the cream. Reduce this a little to thicken it, and pour it over the partridge on serving. Serves 2.

3

Partridge aux Choux

The best way with partridge *aux choux* is to use old birds for the preliminary cooking and at the end to remove these and substitute two young ones which have first been roasted and then buried in the cabbage for a final half-hour. In this way you get a superbly flavoured cabbage and a tender partridge, in fact the best of both worlds.

½ lb bacon	thyme
1 small cabbage	½ bay leaf
water	2 old partridges
salt and pepper	2 oz butter
1 onion (small)	2 cups stock
1 clove	6–8 sausages (small)
parsley	grated nutmeg

Line a casserole or stewpan with rashers of bacon, blanch some cabbage by boiling it for ten minutes, then take it out of the pan, leave it in cold water for five minutes, drain it very well, pressing as much moisture as you can from it with your hands, and put it into the lined stewpan with a seasoning of salt and pepper, the onion with a clove in it, and a bouquet of parsley, thyme, and half a bayleaf. Meanwhile brown the partridges all over in butter, and now bury them in the cabbage, cover with a few more rashers of bacon, add the good stock, put a piece of buttered paper over, then the lid on the pan, bring to the boil, and cook very slowly indeed for at least two hours. Half an hour before you want this dish, put in a few small sausages and a grating or so of nutmeg. Serve the cabbage in a heap, with the sausages and birds, cut in halves, upon it. Serves 4.

Boiled Partridge

The uninitiated may think that this recipe applies to an old bird (*perdrix*) and that it would be gastronomically irreligious to treat a young bird (*perdreau*) in so cavalier a manner. But it is a young 'un that we want and if the recipe is carefully followed, you will have one of the most tender and gamy-flavoured birds that it is possible to serve. A few dwarf Cos lettuce leaves and a bottle of claret and you have a meal for a prince.

1 partridge	½ lb fat bacon rashers
salt	water
6–8 vine leaves	

Salt the bird inside and out, wrap it in vine leaves, and then in thin rashers of fat bacon, and boil it for thirty-five minutes in plain water, putting it in, of course, when the water is boiling. You must then immediately plunge it into iced water, and as soon as it is cold, take it out. The wrappings must be removed when it is served. Serves 2.

Partridges en Casserole

This dish owes some of its flavour to the sausage stuffing, and it would be wicked to waste a young bird on it.

3 oz bacon	½ lb sausage-meat
2 onions (medium)	2 oz butter
2 carrots	1 gill stock
2 old partridges	salt and pepper

Cut some cubes of lean bacon, and fry them for about twenty minutes with chopped onion and carrot. Do not let them brown; let them stew rather. Now stuff the old partridges with sausage-meat, put a piece of fat bacon over each, and brown them all over in butter. Put them in the casserole with carrot, onion, bacon, a few spoonfuls of good stock, and a seasoning of salt and pepper. Cover closely, and cook for at least two hours. Serve as they are. If necessary add more stock. Serves 4.

PHEASANT A LA NORMANDE

The wedding of a young hen pheasant with cream and apple may seem odd enough to some, but it is a good combination nevertheless. Do not attempt, however, to eat this cold; it is not at all nice.

1 pheasant	6 apples (medium)
1½–2 oz butter	½ gill cream

Brown the bird all over in butter, and while this is going on, cut the apples in quarters, peel and core them, and mince them. Then toss them in butter and put a layer of them in the bottom of the pan in which the bird will be cooked, an earthenware *terrine* being the best, as then you can serve the pheasant in it. Lay the pheasant on the bed of apple, and put the rest round it. Pour over it a few spoonfuls of cream, put the lid on the *terrine*, and cook in the oven for half an hour or so. Guinea fowl can be cooked very successfully in the same way. Serves 4.

POTTED GROUSE

This makes a marvellous breakfast dish followed by a fresh peach or, as some prefer, one or two green figs, an aspect of this superfine bird which is sometimes overlooked.

1 pair grouse	½ teaspoon mace
salt and pepper	½ teaspoon grated nutmeg
½ teaspoon ground cloves	6 oz butter

Draw and clean the old grouse very carefully, dry them well, and season them inside and out with a mixture of salt, pepper and ground cloves, mace and grated nutmeg. Then cook them in butter, breast downwards, in a casserole made airtight with a flour and water paste. This should be done in a slow oven and will take anything up to three hours according to their age. When they are done, drain them on a sieve, and cut off all the meat, removing skin and tendons. Put slices of the meat into *terrines* or jars, pressing the layers well down and pouring some melted butter over each one. When full, cover with clarified butter, and they will keep fresh for some weeks in a cold place or the refrigerator. But be careful that in the potting you do not use any of the butter or gravy from the cooking, only the meat and fresh butter.

POUSSINS POLONAISES

A very pleasant way of dealing with baby chickens, to which the Polish garnish of egg, parsley and breadcrumbs lends distinction.

4 *poussins*	bayleaf
6 oz veal	2 oz breadcrumbs
3 oz bacon	½ gill stock
chicken livers	3 oz butter
1 small onion	2 egg-yolks
parsley	2 tablespoons white breadcrumbs
thyme	

Stuff some small *poussins* with a forcemeat made of minced veal, bacon, the chickens' own livers, a little onion, parsley, a touch of thyme and a pinch of powdered bayleaf mixed with breadcrumbs first soaked in stock and a little melted butter. Fry the stuffed birds all over in butter and finish cooking them in a *cocotte* in a moderate oven. When done, cut them downwards in halves and keep them hot, sprinkling them with chopped parsley mixed with the chopped hard-boiled egg-yolks. Now fry a couple of tablespoonfuls of white breadcrumbs, not too fine, in foaming butter for a minute or two, and on serving, pour these quickly over the chicken halves. Serves 4.

RABLE DE LIEVRE ALLEMANDE

We are devotees in these islands of roast and jugged hare, but it is sometimes almost too savoury. This German fashion with the *râble* with its delicate flavour of rosemary may well appeal to those who do not know it already. The *râble* is an extended saddle, from the base of the tail to the neck.

1 *râble* of hare
½ lb quartered mushrooms lightly fried in butter
½ lb bacon strips lightly fried
½ lb button onions glazed

½ bottle red wine
1½ pints of *demi-glace* or glossy brown sauce
¼ pint of blood

Fry the hare, add wine and simmer gently until the wine is reduced to half. Add the brown sauce and either simmer on top of the stove or leave in a casserole in a medium oven until the hare is tender (approximately one and a half hours). Take out the meat and arrange on a serving dish. Meanwhile, thicken the sauce with blood and check seasoning – if necessary, add more salt and plenty of freshly ground black pepper. Arrange the warmed bacon, mushrooms and onions round the *râble* and strain the sauce over the meat. Serve with buttered *pasta* and stewed apples. Serves 6 to 8.

VEGETABLES

ASPARAGUS A LA CREME

Those who find asparagus cooked in the ordinary way rather a messy business to eat will probably, if they do not mind the richness, prefer the creamy way advocated below. Serve with rectangular *croûtons* of toast or with *fleurons* of pastry, which might be cheese-flavoured.

1 bunch asparagus
1½ oz butter
½–1 gill cream

salt and pepper
grated nutmeg (optional)

Cook the asparagus in the usual way and, when well drained, cut the soft part of the heads into pieces about an inch long. (It is just as well, by the way, to keep the asparagus rather under-done for the first part of its cooking.) Keep them hot while you melt a piece of butter in a saucepan, add to it plenty of cream, and season with salt, pepper and, if you like, the tiniest grating of nutmeg. Bring the cream and butter to the boil, then add the asparagus, and shake over the heat for a minute or two longer, until the sauce thickens. Do not stir it or you may break the asparagus pieces. Serves 4.

BEIGNETS DE CHOUX-FLEURS

The Italians have a pleasant way with fish and meat which they call a *fritto misto*. These little cauliflowerets might well make part of this, though they will make a notable dish on their own, when a cheese or *Hollandaise* sauce could be handed with them.

1 cauliflower	parsley
2–3 dessertspoons olive oil	¾ pint batter
lemon juice	oil for frying
salt and pepper	

These are a delicacy for which it is worth while cooking a cauliflower specially. Do not overcook it, so that the flower remains firm though cooked. Separate the little flowerets when they are cold, and let them lie for half an hour in a marinade of olive oil seasoned with lemon juice, salt, pepper and chopped parsley, turning them once or twice. Then drain them, dip them in a good fritter batter and fry them in deep hot oil. Drain them on a cloth, and sprinkle them with salt. This method is also good with asparagus tips, salsify and globe artichokes. Serves 4.

ENDIVES A LA FLAMANDE

In France what we call chicory is known as *endive*, so that this dish must be made with those long white objects which the greengrocer will sell you under the name of chicory. This attractive vegetable is seldom cooked in this country, being confined to its use as a salad. But it offers an excellent cake in the manner described below, which makes it a particularly good companion to roast lamb or mutton.

2 lb endives	salt
1½–2 oz butter	

Prepare them by removing discoloured leaves, scooping out the hard part of the root, and cutting the vegetables across in rounds about the thickness of your finger. Wash them, and dry them in a cloth. Now butter the bottom and sides of a stewpan or casserole just large enough to hold them when they are well pressed down, put the rounds into it, put a circle of buttered paper on top of them, cover tightly, and cook in a slow oven for at least two hours. By then all the liquid from the *endives* should have evaporated, so that you should now be able to turn them out like a cake, quite compact and slightly browned. Just sprinkle this with salt, and serve it. Serves 4.

FRENCH FRIED ONIONS

Nothing like those soggy and greasy slices which often masquerade as fried onions at home, this American designated version is far better to serve as a garnish to a grill in company with the *Basque* tomatoes on page 81, and a few sprigs of watercress as well.

3–4 onions	1 egg white
2 oz flour	cooking fat

Cut the onions into thin rings, dip these in flour, then in beaten white of egg, then in flour again, and fry them in deep fat. Serves 4.

GRATIN DE COURGETTES

When we first went to live in the country in 1932, the real *courgette* was grown here only by the vegetable specialist, so we used in its place the tiny baby marrows from a vegetable marrow plant. This elegant dish with cheese is just the thing for a summer luncheon when they proliferate, and is usually a surprise.

1½ lb baby marrows	1 gill single cream
water	3 oz cheese
salt and pepper	1 egg
1 oz butter	

Take some small marrows about three inches long, scrape them lightly, chop them up finely, and put them into a wide saucepan with just enough water to prevent their catching, about a tablespoonful. Add a pinch of salt, and stir and cook them until all the water has evaporated.

Then add a little butter, some thin cream, grated cheese, and an egg. Mix, pepper lightly, and pour into a shallow fireproof dish. Sprinkle liberally with grated cheese, dot with butter, and brown quickly in the oven. Serves 4.

HARICOT BEANS

It is so much better to cook our haricot beans ourselves, plainly, than to buy the tomato-flavoured tinned kind, that the few hints below may be found useful. As a schoolboy I had a passion for them and I think I still have.

½ lb haricot beans	parsley
water	thyme
salt and pepper	bayleaf
1 carrot	1½ oz butter
1 onion	lemon juice
1–2 cloves	

It is worth while being reminded every now and then of the French way of cooking haricot beans, the only right way in my opinion. Do not soak the beans overnight: two hours in warm water should be sufficient, if they are in good condition. Drain them, then put them into a pan, preferably of earthenware, and cover them well with warm water. Bring them gently to the boil on a moderate heat, and then take the pan from the heat and leave it for about an hour, when the beans should be nicely swollen. Pour off the water and throw it away (it has a most unpleasant smell and is useless for anything), put the beans back into the pan once more and cover them this time with salted boiling water, adding a carrot cut in four, an onion stuck with a clove or two and a bouquet of parsley, thyme and bayleaf. Cover the pan again, and let it cook on a very gentle heat for an hour and a half. The beans can then be drained, and the liquid reserved for the excellent stock it is. The best way to serve the beans now is to shake them over a good heat so that they dry, then take the pan off the heat and add a good piece of butter, pepper, salt if necessary, a squeeze of lemon juice and some chopped parsley. Just shake the pan to dissolve the butter and mix the other seasonings with the beans: on no account must the butter cook or its delicious fresh flavour will be lost. Serves 4.

HORS D'ŒUVRES

Leeks à la Grecque

One of the very nicest vegetable *hors d'œuvres.*

1½ lb leeks	1 tomato
water	parsley
salt and pepper	thyme
saffron	bayleaf
1 shallot	olive oil

The leeks should be smallish and all of the same size, and they should first be cooked gently in salted water until they are tender, but not at all broken. Then drain them and lay them in a shallow fireproof dish with a seasoning of salt, pepper, and saffron. Add a chopped shallot and the flesh of a tomato cut up small, a bouquet of parsley, thyme, and bayleaf, and enough olive oil to come level with the top of the leeks. Bring to the boil and cook for three or four minutes only. Remove the bouquet at once, and let this agreeable dish get cold. Serves 4.

If something stronger is wanted try this, which came from the old Café Monico in Shaftesbury Avenue. Some chefs like to add a few button mushrooms to it, but it used to make a regular appearance on the *hors d'œuvre* trolleys of the West End.

Onions Monegasque

1 lb onions (small)	salt and pepper
½ pint water	2 oz sultanas
2 port glasses wine vinegar (white)	parsley
3 tablespoons olive oil	thyme
3 tablespoons tomato *purée*	bayleaf
1½ oz castor sugar	

Put the peeled onions into a stewpan with the water, vinegar, olive oil, tomato *purée*, castor sugar, a little freshly ground pepper and salt, the sultanas, and a bouquet of parsley, thyme, and bayleaf. Bring to the boil and cook very gently for about an hour and a half with the lid on. Take out the bouquet when the onions are cold. Serves 4.

LETTUCE A L'ETOUFFEE

We have already had a LETTUCE SOUP (see page 15), and here is a way of cooking it to eat with veal or lamb. With care it can be made with lettuces that are beginning to bolt, but you must see that you do not use the stalk or ribs or it will be bitter.

1 lb lettuce	1 lump sugar (small)
1½–2 oz butter	4 onions (small)
parsley	salt
thyme	½ oz flour
bayleaf	

Wash and drain the lettuce leaves, and cut them across in strips of about a finger's width. (I have found myself that in this dish Cos lettuces are better.) Divide an ounce of butter into little pieces. Put a third of the lettuce into a stewpan which has been previously buttered, put on it a third of the butter, then lettuce and butter until the other two-thirds have been put in, in two more layers. In the middle on top put a bouquet of parsley, thyme, and bayleaf, the sugar, and small onions. Sprinkle lightly with salt, but do not add any liquid whatsoever. Now cover the pan closely, and let the contents simmer for three-quarters of an hour to an hour. When the lettuce is done, there will be a couple of tablespoonfuls or so of liquid left in the bottom of the pan, and this you can bind quickly with flour and butter and pour over the lettuce, which you will serve with the onions, if you like, but with the bouquet removed. Serves 4.

ONION RAGOUT

After the destruction of Smyrna, when so many English merchants fled to England, I used to lunch with some of them in a little restaurant near the Pump at Aldgate. Among other Middle Eastern dishes an Onion *Ragoût* was specially inveigling, and I have copied it down from what the restaurateur told me.

2 lb onions (small)	1 stick cinnamon (small)
2 oz butter	2 bayleaves
2 tablespoons white wine	½ pint stock
cloves	½ lb tomatoes

Put the onions into a stewpan with the butter, and fry them a golden brown. Then add the white wine, a few cloves, the cinnamon, and bayleaves. Moisten with good stock, and add the tomatoes rubbed through a fine sieve. Simmer all together for about an hour, or until the onions are tender, and serve hot. Serves 4.

PETITS POIS A LA FRANCAISE

Do not think that because of the cooking instructions old peas can be used here. On the contrary, the sweeter and smallest should be chosen, and if your aim is perfection, see that they are all of the same size.

1½ pints peas	3 lumps sugar
1 lettuce heart	water
12 button onions	4 sprigs parsley
3 oz butter	1 sprig summer savory (optional)

Put the shelled peas in a thick enamel saucepan with the heart of a small cabbage lettuce cut in half, the onions cleaned but not peeled, two and a half ounces of butter, and the sugar broken into small pieces. Mix these well together, and leave in a cool place with a cover over them for an hour. When you are ready to cook the peas, add half a dozen tablespoonfuls of cold water and a bouquet of four sprigs of parsley tied together with, if possible, a sprig of summer savory. Cover the pan with a soup plate – with half a cupful of cold water in it – so that it fits well down on to the pan. Now put the pan on an even heat, and when its contents come to the boil, move it to the side of the heat (or on to a low flame under an asbestos or other mat). The peas must poach, not simmer. If they cook too fast or too long they will mash. Allow eight to ten minutes for them to come to the boil and twenty-five minutes afterwards. During their cooking, renew the water in the soup plate two or three times (when it begins to get appreciably hot), and shake the pan now and again, but do not stir the peas with a spoon. At the end of this time there should be only about a tablespoonful of liquid left. Two or three minutes before serving take out the bouquet, and put the onions and lettuce on a plate to keep warm. Toss the peas over the heat, so that the remaining liquid reduces, and then add half an ounce of butter in small pieces, shaking it carefully into the peas.

Now put them into a dish, and arrange the lettuce and onions around them, so that you can distribute these 'extras' among those who like them. Serves 4.

POTATOES

These five potato dishes provide, each in its own way, a superfine addition to a main course, though the dish from the *Dauphiné* can well stand alone as a separate course. It is controversial whether the cheese should be omitted, but I think not, for English tastes, as without it the impact of the garlic may be too much for British palates.

Martinique Potatoes

4 baked potatoes
¾ tablespoon butter
3 tablespoons cream (off the milk)

salt and pepper
grated nutmeg
1 egg

Sieve the pulp of the baked potatoes or put it through a ricer, and add the butter, cream, salt, pepper, grated nutmeg, and the slightly beaten egg-yolk. Stir over the heat for two or three minutes, then add by degrees the stiffly whisked egg-white. Shape like meringues between two greased tablespoons, and bake on a greased sheet until delicately browned. Serves 4.

Pommes Dauphinoise

2½ lb potatoes
2 oz butter
1 clove garlic
salt and pepper

grated nutmeg
1 pint milk
1 egg
2 oz *Gruyère* cheese

Peel and slice your potatoes thinly, and arrange them in layers in a fireproof dish which you have first rubbed round with a cut clove of garlic and then well buttered. Sprinkle each layer with salt, pepper, and a little grated nutmeg. When the dish is getting full, pour in the

milk into which you have beaten an egg and a couple of ounces of grated
Gruyère cheese. Sprinkle the top with more grated cheese, and cook in a
moderate oven for about an hour. Serves 4.

Pommes Limousine

1½ lb potatoes   1 oz fat
3 oz bacon

Peel and grate the potatoes coarsely and mix in with them some very
small dice of fat bacon. Heat some fat in a frying-pan until smoking
hot, then put in the potato mixture, flattening it all over the pan. Cook
until one side is browned, then turn it over and brown the other. The
thinner and crisper it is the better. Use a large frying-pan. Serves 4.

Sandy Potatoes

1 lb potatoes   2 tablespoons breadcrumbs
2 oz butter

The potatoes should be pared and then cut in dice of about one-inch
sides. They must then be fried slowly in shallow butter and, when
both sides are golden, some white breadcrumbs are added towards the
end and cooked with them. The crumbs adhere to the potato dice,
with the result that they are as if sandy when done. Serves 4.

Potatoes with Cheese

1½ lb potatoes   4 oz *Gruyère* cheese
salt and pepper   1 cup stock
grated nutmeg   butter

Chop up very finely some raw peeled potatoes and season them with
salt, pepper, and grated nutmeg. Butter a shallow fireproof dish, put
in a layer of potatoes, and cover it with a layer of grated *Gruyère* cheese.
Then more potatoes and more cheese. Moisten with good stock, dot
with butter, and put on the top of the stove until the stock boils. When
it has boiled for ten minutes, put the dish in the oven and cook it until
the top is golden and all the stock has disappeared. Floury potatoes are
best for this dish, and at a pinch a mild Cheddar could be used.
Serves 4.

RED CABBAGE POLONAISE

Until I had reached the age of sixteen, the only thing I thought one did with red cabbage was to pickle it. To eat it hot with, say, a knuckle of pork was an experience worth waiting for.

1 red cabbage (medium)
water
1 apple
½ oz butter
1 tablespoon onion
1 saltspoon salt
cayenne

grated nutmeg
1 dessertspoon brown sugar
1 tablespoon vinegar (or 2 tablespoons red wine)
1 pinch powdered cloves
1 pinch powdered cinnamon

Cut the cabbage in shreds as for pickling, and let these lie in cold water for half an hour. Put them in handfuls straight from the water into a saucepan, adding a peeled, cored, and sliced apple, the butter, chopped onion, salt, a dash of cayenne, and a little grated nutmeg; do not add any liquid. Cover closely, and cook slowly for about an hour, until the cabbage is tender. Then stir in the brown sugar, vinegar (or, in my own private version, the red wine), and a pinch of powdered cloves and cinnamon. Finish cooking with the lid on for ten minutes longer. It is delicious. Serves 4.

SALSIFY A LA NORMANDE

In English cookery books salsify used to be called the vegetable oyster. Why, I am not quite sure for its flavour has no connection with that glorious bivalve. I rather think it was because the usual sauce made to accompany it was quite possibly an anchovy one, which imparted to it the fishy taste. Be that as it may, the exquisite *Sauce Normande* is far better than anything else can be.

1½ lb salsify
2 oz butter
1 onion
1 tablespoon flour
½–1 gill cider

salt and pepper
grated nutmeg (or cinnamon)
1 gill cream
lemon juice

Boil the salsify in the usual way, but instead of serving it with a white sauce use the following *Sauce Normande*. Melt a large nut of butter over a gentle heat, and in it lightly brown an onion chopped very finely. Add another piece of butter and the flour, and let them cook a little together. Moisten with cider, stirring well and adding some more tiny pieces of butter. Season with salt, pepper, and a little grated nutmeg or cinnamon and, just before serving, whip in some fresh cream with a squeeze of lemon juice at the very last. Serves 4.

SWEET CORN

Sweet Corn is encountered *au nature* and tinned in the shops today. Here are two different ways of using both.

Corn on the Cob

4 sweet corn cobs   butter
water

Many people grow sweet corn and then wonder what to do with it. Strip off the husk and silky parts. Plunge the cobs into boiling water, put on the lid, and boil for ten or fifteen minutes. Be careful not to salt the water, as it hardens the corn. Eat with melted butter, sticking a fork into each end of the cob and biting off the corn with your teeth. Serves 4.

Corn Oysters

2 breakfast cups sweet corn   2 tablespoons milk
   (tinned) $\frac{3}{4}$ cup cracker crumbs
$1\frac{1}{2}$ teaspoons salt   1 egg
pepper   bacon fat

Put the tinned corn into a saucepan, bring to the boil, and simmer for a quarter of an hour. Then add the salt, some pepper, the milk, cracker crumbs, and the well-beaten egg. Mix well together and drop, a spoonful at a time, into a frying-pan containing a little hot bacon fat. When both sides are nicely browned, the 'oysters' are ready. Serves 4.

TOMATOES

The stuffed tomatoes from the South of France are an example of dealing with them as a complicated dish whereas that from the *Basque* country shows, to my mind, the perfect method of making them fit for a simple garnish, say to a grilled chop or steak.

Antibes Tomatoes

1 tin anchovy fillets (small)	8–12 tomatoes (medium)
garlic	salt and pepper
1 tin tunny fish (small)	thyme
2 tablespoons finely chopped *fines herbes*	parsley
	fennel
3 oz breadcrumbs	olive oil
1½ teaspoons milk	toast (or fried bread)

Pound up some anchovy fillets with a touch of garlic, a little tinned tunny fish carefully drained of oil, some *fines herbes* (parsley, chervil, chives, and tarragon), and a small amount of breadcrumbs soaked in milk and then drained. Scoop out some tomato halves and fill them with this mixture, sprinkle each one lightly with salt, pepper, a little chopped thyme, parsley and fennel, and finally a few drops of olive oil. Bake them in the oven, and serve them on toast or fried bread. Serves 4.

Fried Tomatoes Basquaise

8 tomatoes	parsley
olive oil	

Halve the tomatoes crosswise and scoop out the juice and pips only. Cover the bottom of the frying-pan with olive oil, and as soon as it smokes put in the tomatoes cut side downwards. Cook on a good heat until they are slightly scorched, and serve sprinkled with chopped parsley. Serves 4.

PUDDINGS

APPLES

No fruit makes a better pudding than the apple, and they are with us from an early age. As we grow older and emerge from nursery days, our puddings vary from the simplicity of a jelly to plain sections spiced with cinnamon and suet-encased fruit and then to the sophistication of the French way with an apple pudding and lastly its apotheosis in a red wine and stuffed with pineapple and deep-fat fried as they serve it in the United States.

Apple and Greengage Mould

1 lb apples	1 pint packet greengage jelly
2 oz sugar	$\frac{1}{2}$ pint double cream
$\frac{1}{4}$ pint water	

Cook the peeled, cored and sliced apples with the sugar and water until they are soft, then whip them up with a fork until they are smooth and frothy. In this dissolve the jelly cut into very small pieces. Pour into a mould to set, and decorate with whipped cream. Serves 4.

Apples in Wine

2 lb apples   4 oz castor sugar
1½–2 oz butter   1 glass red wine (large)

Peel, core, and cut some apples (they must be the kind that melt
readily when cooked) into thin slices and lay them in overlapping rows
or rings in a fairly deep buttered dish sprinkling each layer liberally
with castor sugar. Fill the dish to the brim and pour over the wine.
Put on a lid or plate, pressing it well down, and cook in a slow oven for
four hours. By that time the apples will be a lovely deep red and become
a jelly for serving. Serves 4.

Apples Lexington

6 sharp cooking apples   breadcrumbs
1 oz flour   fat
1 oz castor sugar   pineapple (or other fruit)
1 egg

Peel and core the rather sour cooking apples, and steam them until
they are half-cooked. Let them get cold, then roll them in a mixture
of flour and castor sugar, brush them all over with beaten egg and coat
them with stale breadcrumbs. Fry them in deep fat to a rich gold, then
fill the centres with finely chopped pineapple or other chosen fruit
filling, serving them hot with a syrup from the stuffing fruit poured
round them. Serves 4.

Apples with Cinnamon

1½ lb apples   1 teaspoon powdered cinnamon or
1½–2 oz butter   more to taste
3 oz sugar   stale plain cake

Peel and core the apples and cut them into thinnish sections. Fry these
very gently in a little butter until they are soft and browned on each
side. Then scatter over them some sugar mixed with a pinch or two
of powdered cinnamon, cook on a few minutes longer, and serve hot,
garnished with strips of fried stale plain cake. Serves 4.

Baked Apple Pudding

½ oz fat   1½ lb apples
suet crust: lemon juice
   1 lb self-raising flour   4 oz sugar
   4–5 oz suet   1½ tablespoons golden syrup
   ¾ gill water   1 tablespoon brown sugar

Grease a Yorkshire pudding-tin well, and line it with a thin layer of
suet crust. On this put a thick layer of peeled and chopped apples,
and sprinkle these with lemon juice and sugar. Cover with another
thin layer of the crust, spread the top with golden syrup, and sprinkle
brown sugar over it. Bake until the top crust is brown and crisp, and
eat with gratitude. It is advisable to cook this on a baking tray in case
the syrup runs over the raised edge of the pie. Serves 4.

Normandy Pudding

6 cooking apples   4 eggs
6 oz breadcrumbs   1 lemon
salt   1 glass rum (or brandy)
1 teaspoon powdered cinnamon   butter
4 oz castor sugar   wine sauce

Chop up, fairly coarsely, the peeled and cored cooking apples, and stir
them up in a bowl with the breadcrumbs, a pinch of salt, the powdered
cinnamon, and castor sugar. Add gradually the beaten eggs and, when
all are well mixed, stir in the juice and grated rind of a lemon and the
rum or brandy. Put into a well-buttered mould or basin, cover with
buttered paper and a cloth, and steam for about two hours. Serve a
wine sauce with it. Serves 4.

BAKED ORANGES

We seldom think of this simple and always welcome way with oranges,
which can be served hot or cold. Ripe quinces can be prepared in the
same manner, and turn a lovely deep red in the process.

3 oranges (large)   2 teaspoons cornflour (level)
water   1 teacup orange juice
3 oz granulated sugar   1 teacup water
½ sherry glass brandy   brandy
½ oz butter

Wash the oranges (preferably seedless), cover them with boiling water, and cook them until the skin is tender. Drain, cut in halves across, remove the cores and arrange the halves, cut side upwards, in a baking dish. Fill the centre of each with granulated sugar, sprinkle sugar over the flesh and, if you can, pour a few drops of brandy in each before adding a few thin flakes of butter. Bake until the sugar melts and browns slightly, and serve them warm with the following sauce: cook the cornflour in a teacupful of water and the same of orange juice for three minutes, and flavour at the last with a few drops of brandy. Serves 4.

BANANAS

Banana Cream Pie

Apart from baking bananas with sugar and rum, this is as good as any way of making a cream pie so much affected by Americans.

6 oz pastry	$\frac{1}{2}$ pint custard
5–6 bananas	$1\frac{1}{2}$ gills double cream
lemon juice	

Make a flan case of your best pastry and, when it is cold, fill it with overlapping slices of banana, sprinkling them as you go with a little lemon juice. Cover these with an ordinary boiled custard, and finish with whipped cream. Serves 4.

Fried Bananas

8 bananas	1 egg
2 oz sugar	clarified butter (for frying)
1 lemon (juice only)	1 glass rum (small)

Cut the bananas in halves lengthways after peeling them, and let them lie for a little while sprinkled with sugar and lemon juice. They should not be over-ripe or they will be difficult to handle. Then drain and dip in a well-whisked egg, and fry in clarified butter, which should take about five minutes. Arrange them then on a hot dish and just before serving, throw over them the warmed rum, and set it alight. Serves 4.

BONDE PIGE

This Scandinavian sweet was introduced to us by an old friend who lived in a little cottage in Kingsclere near Newbury. It is a pleasant enough novelty, and the name means 'Peasant Girl with Veil', though which is the girl and which the veil I have yet to discover.

8–10 oz brown bread	$\frac{1}{4}$–$\frac{1}{2}$ pint apple *purée*
3–4 oz butter	4 tablespoons raspberry jam
2 oz sugar	$\frac{1}{2}$ pint double cream

Crumble some stale brown bread, spread it on a baking-tin, and bake it in the oven with butter and a little sugar sifted over it. Stir it now and again to keep the crumbs separate, and keep your eye on it or it may burn suddenly. While it is still hot, spread a layer in a dish, cover it with a layer of thick apple *purée*, then with raspberry jam and then more of the crumbs. Repeat these layers and, when the sweet is cold, cover the top with plenty of whipped cream. Serves 4.

CHERRIES IN CLARET

When making this dish, it will contribute to the comfort of all if the cherry-stones are first removed. What the fruit loses in flavour is absorbed by the juice.

2 lb cherries	$\frac{1}{4}$ teaspoon powdered cinnamon
$\frac{1}{2}$ bottle claret	1 tablespoon redcurrant jelly
2 oz sugar or more to taste	

Put the cherries in a saucepan with enough claret to cover them, adding sugar to taste and a tiny pinch of powdered cinnamon. Bring slowly to the boil, and immediately it shows signs of boiling draw the pan to the side of the stove, or on to a lower heat, and let the cherries just poach for ten minutes or so with the lid on. When they are cold, stir in the melted redcurrant jelly. Serves 4.

COMPOTE OF GOOSEBERRIES

This is a recipe which will serve as an example of all good *compôtes*. The addition of the Kirsch makes all the difference.

1 quart gooseberries	1 tablespoon apricot jam
water	1 liqueurglass Kirsch
$\frac{1}{2}$ lb sugar	

Top and tail the green gooseberries, put them into a saucepan (or better, an earthenware casserole) of boiling water and scald them for a couple of minutes. Now, in another saucepan, make a syrup by boiling the sugar in a pint of water for ten minutes, then add the drained gooseberries, apricot jam, and Kirsch. Simmer the fruit until tender; let it grow cold in the syrup, and serve as cold as possible. Serves 4.

COUPE CLO-CLO: PINCH PIE

Two beautiful sweets for summer-time, the first an ice cream named, I suppose, after a nineteenth-century actress or courtesan, who certainly had good taste, and the other given to me some time ago by the Canadian wife of an editor.

Coupe Clo-Clo

12 *marrons glacés*	½ pint vanilla ice cream
1 wineglass Maraschino (or Kirsch)	½ pint double cream
	2 tablespoons strawberry *purée*

Break up a few *marrons glacés*, soak them for a little in Maraschino or Kirsch, and then mix them with a vanilla ice cream. In the bottom of each cup put a layer of the *marrons*, cover this generously with the ice cream, and surmount it by a whole *marron* surrounded by a piped border of whipped cream flavoured with strawberry *purée*. Serves 4.

Pinch Pie

1 teaspoon water	½ teaspoon baking powder
1 teaspoon white vinegar	butter
1 teaspoon vanilla essence	flour
3 egg-whites	¾ lb quick frozen strawberries (or raspberries)
4½ oz icing sugar	
⅛ teaspoon salt	½ pint double cream

First of all mix together in a small cup the water, good white vinegar and vanilla essence. Now whisk the egg-whites until they are stiff, and add very slowly, half a teaspoonful at a time, the icing sugar, finely sieved and mixed with the salt and baking powder. As you beat in the sugar, add alternately with it a few drops of the mixture in the cup, and when all has been added, go on beating the mixture for several minutes. Now butter and flour a flan tin, heap the meringue mixture upon it, and shape it like a tart with a spatula. Bake it in a very slow oven until crisp, and when ready to serve, fill it with well-drained quick-frozen strawberries or raspberries, and coat it with whipped cream. Serves 4.

CREMES

Crême Brulée

This lovely rich custard encased in its crunchy covering of caramel is a highlight among the many young cooks who have discovered it. In a year particularly good for hazelnuts an old friend walked seven or eight miles to us, there and back, for the sole purpose of getting from us the recipe for CRÊME DE NOISETTES, which when made with the freshly gathered creamy nuts is indeed something to talk about.

1 pint cream	8 egg-yolks
1 stick cinnamon	3 oz castor sugar
1 piece lemon rind (small)	cream (optional)

Put an ounce of sugar, a stick of cinnamon, and the lemon rind into the cream. Bring slowly to the boil, and add, off the heat, the well beaten and strained yolks of egg. Do this by degrees, whipping all the time, but on no account allowing the mixture to boil. Now pour it into a shallow fireproof dish, and bake it like a custard in a pan of hot water in the oven. When it is cooked, let it get quite cold, then cover it with a thick layer of castor sugar. Put the dish under the grill and brown the sugar so that it caramelises. Put it by to cool, and decorate it, if you like, with whipped cream. Serves 4.

Crême de Noisettes

½ pint milk	water
4 oz hazelnuts	4 egg-yolks
4 sheets gelatine (or ½ oz powdered gelatine)	¼ lb castor sugar
	½ pint cream

Bring the milk to the boil, and then, off the heat, add to it the finely chopped grilled hazelnuts. Bring to the boil again, put on the lid, and cook thus for a few minutes. Now add the sheets of gelatine – softened in cold water (not quite ½ oz powdered gelatine) – after the liquid has cooled a little, and add, too, the yolks of four eggs, well mixed with the castor sugar. Let the mixture thicken quietly on a slow heat, stirring all the time, and then let it get cold. Then add the whipped cream, put it into a mould, and leave it on ice or in the refrigerator for a couple of hours before you want it. Serves 4.

CREPE DU COUVENT

This pancake with pears is very good indeed. It could, of course, be made with tinned pears, but they would have to be well-drained first.

1½ gills pancake batter   2–3 pears (cooked or tinned)
fat

Make some pancake batter, pour half of it into your frying-pan, suitably greased, and cook until the underside is lightly browned. Then scatter over the uncooked side some dice of cooked pears, pour the rest of the batter over the top, and finish cooking in the oven. Turn out upside-down to serve. Serves 4.

DUKE OF CAMBRIDGE TART

This was, and no doubt still is, a feature of the strictly English meals served at the Hind's Head at Bray. I am assured that when the Queen once went there to luncheon she asked for treacle tart as a special favourite but the eggy crystallised fruit taste of this dish is very much to be preferred, I think.

pastry   3 oz castor sugar
2 oz candied peel (or crystallised   3 oz butter
   fruits)   2 egg-yolks

Line a flan ring with pastry, chop up finely the candied peel or crystallised fruits and scatter them over the paste. Now put into a small saucepan the castor sugar, melted butter, and the egg-yolks. Stir and cook, and when the mixture boils pour it over the peel in the flan. Then bake in a slack oven until the top is a rich, crinkly brown. If the mixture does not boil the top will not crinkle as it should. Serves 4.

PEARS, STUFFED

This delicious amalgam of fresh pears and *marrons glacés* laced with a liqueur of your choice makes one of the finest sweets that a hostess could devise.

2 ripe pears
8-12 *marrons glacés*
¾-1 pint cream

2-3 teaspoons *Curaçao* (or *Grand Marnier* or *Cointreau*)

Peel and core some good dessert pears and fill the hollow of each half with *marrons glacés* broken in small pieces. Then mask each pear with whipped cream flavoured with either *Curaçao*, *Grand Marnier* or *Cointreau*, and serve chilled. Tins of *marron glacé debris* can be bought for this and similar purposes. Serves 4.

PINEAPPLE

These three pineapple sweets are as good in their way as any. The pineapple in wine makes a fancy dish and the recipe with the *Sauternes* is remarkable. At one period of the year very small and very ripe fruit may be bought and these, hollowed out and filled with ice cream and then topped with Kirsch-flavoured whipped cream, make a party dish well worth thinking of.

Pineapple in Melon

1 melon (green or yellow)
1 pint sugar syrup (depending on the size of the melon)
3-4 teaspoons ginger

¾ pint cream
1 fresh pineapple (or 1 medium tin)

Peel an oblong green or yellow melon, cut it in half lengthwise, take out the seeds, put the halves together again, and soak them for a couple of hours in some hot sugar syrup (not the tinned Golden variety), flavoured with ginger. When it is cold, drain it, and stuff it with a mixture of stiffly whipped cream and cubes of pineapple. Serve as cold as possible. Serves 4.

Pineapple Pancake

4 eggs	4 tablespoons cream (thick)
5½ oz sugar	grated nutmeg
1 tablespoon pineapple marmalade	½ oz butter
4 tablespoons flour	

Beat up the egg-yolks with four tablespoonfuls of sugar until very light, then add the pineapple marmalade, flour, thick cream, and a grating of nutmeg. Whisk the whites stiffly, and fold them into the mixture. Melt a piece of butter in an omelette-pan, pour in the mixture, and fry on a slow fire until a light brown underneath. Turn it over on to a dish, sprinkle with fine sugar and, if you like, pass it very quickly under a grill. Serves 4.

Pineapple with Wine

1 pineapple
½ bottle *Sauternes* (sweet)
castor sugar

Remove the core of a fresh pineapple, and pour the wine into it, or as much as will go. Leave this in the pineapple, in a cool place, for a day and a night, then pour off the wine, and serve the sliced pineapple simply with castor sugar. It should be tried for a pleasant experience. Serves 4.

PLAIN PUDDINGS

Two plain puddings from early childhood, the taste for which has never deserted me. Nowadays perhaps a little touch of sophistication has grown in them, say the use of an unusual hot jam with the RAILWAY PUDDING, such as quince, black cherry or gooseberry and a mixture of golden syrup and black treacle with the sponge; but it must not do more than very slightly darken the gold.

Railway Pudding

6 oz flour	milk
1 teaspoon baking powder	vanilla essence
3 oz butter	butter (for greasing the tin)
4 oz castor sugar	jam
1 egg	

Sieve together the flour and baking powder, rub in the butter, and then add three ounces of castor sugar. Beat up an egg with a little milk and mix with the dry ingredients until you have a dropping consistency. Add a few drops of vanilla essence and bake in a greased pie-dish or Yorkshire pudding tin in a moderate oven until just firm and golden-brown. Turn it out, split it, and spread with warm jam. Put the halves together again and either serve as they are or cut into fingers or squares. Sprinkle these with castor sugar and serve. Serves 4.

Treacle Sponge

4½ oz butter	1 wineglass milk
½ lb flour (self-raising)	grated lemon peel (optional)
4 oz sugar	4 tablespoons golden syrup
2 eggs	

Rub four ounces of butter into the flour, add four ounces of sugar (or less, according to taste), and mix with the beaten eggs and milk, adding a little grated lemon peel if you like. Butter a pudding basin and put the golden syrup in the bottom. Turn in the pudding mixture, and steam for an hour and a half to two hours. Serves 4.

QUINCES, BAKED

8 quinces	12 level teaspoons sugar
water	

Beautiful orange-yellow ripe quinces are essential for this unusual sweet. Wash and peel them, core them after cutting them in halves, and lay them, cored side upwards, in a greased fireproof dish in which you will serve them. Boil the peel and cores in enough water to cover them, and after twenty minutes strain off the liquid. Now put a level teaspoonful

and a half of sugar in each quince half, pour over two tablespoonfuls
of the quince liquid, and bake, covered, in a slow oven for about three
hours (owners of heat storage cookers please specially note!) or until
they are quite tender. Marvellous for those who like the quince's
ineffable perfume! Serves 4.

SHERRY CREAM

A really sweet sherry is what is wanted here, though in other cases a
medium is preferable.

1 pint cream	grated lemon rind
1 egg-yolk	sugar
3 tablespoons sherry (sweet)	

Cook the cream with the well beaten egg-yolk, sherry, a touch of grated
lemon rind, and enough sugar to sweeten it as you like it; cook these
all in a double saucepan, or over a very gentle heat. Keep stirring all
the time, and when the mixture assumes the consistency of thick cream,
take the pan off the heat, and continue to stir until it is cold. Serves 4.

SPANISH FRITTERS

These spicy little fritters are very jolly by themselves but could be
happily eaten with some rather thick and syrupy *compôte* of fruit.

2 stale rolls (or any white bread)	powdered cinnamon
cream (or milk)	castor sugar
1 egg	butter (for frying)
grated nutmeg	jam (optional)

Get a French roll, or indeed any stale white bread, remove the crust,
and cut the crumb into rounds as thick as your finger. Soak them in a
little cream or even milk, into which you have beaten an egg, seasoned
with grated nutmeg, powdered cinnamon, and castor sugar. When they
are well soaked, let them dry a little, and then fry them brown in a little
butter, and serve them very hot. Hot jam can be handed with them if
necessary, but better just to give them the faintest powdering with very
fine sugar. Serves 4.

TETE DE NEGRE

In this charming dish the whipped-up softness of the cream turban offers a delightful contrast to the chocolatey rice.

2 oz carolina rice

2 oz sugar

¼ pint milk

½ vanilla pod (or 3 drops essence)

3 egg-yolks

¾ pint double cream

For the sauce:

3 oz plain or cooking chocolate

1 tablespoon water

2 oz butter

Make some vanilla-flavoured cream of rice by boiling the rice in water for two minutes, draining it and finishing the cooking in half a pint of milk. When it is cooked, drain it and add a custard made up of the remaining milk, the egg-yolks and sugar by straining it on to the rice and mixing it well. Let it get cool. Mix in a couple of tablespoonfuls of thick cream, put it all into a water-rinsed pudding-basin, and let it get quite cold. Turn it out when wanted, and mask it with a chocolate sauce, which you can easily make by melting grated chocolate with the warm water and a piece of butter the size of a small hen's egg. When this is cold, whip up some cream stiffly, and arrange it like a turban on the 'head'. Serves 4.

SAVOURIES

CAMEMBERT FRIT

To many this will seem a contradiction in terms and very brusque treatment of this lovely cheese. When I first went to a newly opened London restaurant in the 1930s I ordered this savoury which was unknown to them at the time. Three months later I returned and asked for it again, when a new *maître d'hôtel* exclaimed, 'Ah, you mean what the Prince of Wales has.' Such is fame!

1 *Camembert* cheese

1 teaspoon cayenne

1 egg

2–3 tablespoons breadcrumbs

fat (for frying)

Clear the *Camembert* cheese of its crust, and cut it into elongated lozenges. Sprinkle these with cayenne. Egg-and-breadcrumb them *twice*, and fry at the last minute in hot deep fat. The cheese should not be too ripe, and the second egg-and-breadcrumbing should not be done until the first has dried on well, and the loose crumbs have been shaken off. Serves 4.

CHEESE AIGRETTES

One of the very best of Victorian cheese dishes and a use for *choux* paste apart from the *éclair* and cream bun. It is really quite exquisite, and if some are tempted to hand grated cheese with these little fritters, let them first taste them without this extra accompaniment. The *aigrettes* may be baked, if for digestive reasons the fried ones are unsuitable.

¼ pint water	2 oz cheese
1 oz butter	salt and pepper
2½ oz flour	cayenne
1–2 eggs	fat (or oil, for frying)

Put the water and butter into a saucepan and bring to the boil. Add the flour and beat well until the mixture is smooth and leaves the sides of the pan. Let it cool a little, then add an egg (or better, two) by degrees, beating well all the time. Then add the grated cheese and a seasoning of salt, pepper and a touch of cayenne, but be wary of this last! Drop small teaspoonfuls of this mixture into fat or oil that is just beginning to smoke and in ten to fifteen minutes they will be done. If the fat is too hot the outsides will brown before the insides are cooked, so it is best to try one first by itself, to make sure that the temperature is just right so that they will emerge crisp and golden. Serves 4.

CHEESE BOUCHEES

These little mouthfuls, the size of a penny, often appeared at the Hind's Head at Bray, as a preliminary to one of the remarkable meals served there.

1 tablespoon flour	salt and pepper
1 pint milk	cayenne
3 eggs	1 lb made up rough-puff pastry
6 oz cheese	

Mix the flour smoothly with a little of the milk, and to this add the beaten eggs. Now, in a double saucepan, add the rest of the milk and grated cheese seasoned with salt and pepper, and a touch of cayenne. Heat up over boiling water, and simmer very gently for twenty minutes. Use this mixture to fill tiny pastry cases made with rough-puff pastry, and put them into the oven for a quarter of an hour or so, handing them as hot as possible. Serves 4.

CROQUE-MONSIEUR

Ham and cheese make an admirable combination, as is illustrated in many Italian dishes. The tips here are to have the bread and its filling as thin as is humanly possible and to safeguard against the little sandwiches slipping apart by tying them before frying with a little cotton.

bread	cooked bacon (or ham)
cheese (*Emmentaler* or *Gruyère* is best)	butter

Thin slices, all the same size, must be cut of crustless stale bread, cheese, and lean cooked bacon or ham, one of the last for every two of the others. Make little sandwiches of bread, cheese, ham, cheese and bread, and fry them in very hot butter, so that the bread is golden on each side before the cheese has time to melt and run out. Made with small triangular cheeses the savouries are small enough to turn over in the pan without coming to pieces.

FRIED CHEESE

This is the same as the recipe for FRIED CAMEMBERT on page 95, save that the triangular *Petit Gruyères* are used instead of *Camembert*. But I think that the faint semi-sweetness of the cheese militates against their complete success, although they are easier to get than their more expensive counterpart.

1 box *Petit Gruyère* cheeses	breadcrumbs (browned)
cayenne	fat (for frying)
1 egg	

If the *Petit Gruyère* cheeses are thick ones, cut them in half lengthwise; if thin ones, cut them across. Sprinkle them with a little cayenne, and egg-and-breadcrumb them twice, preferably using white of egg and fine browned breadcrumbs. Then fry them in deep fat until golden and crisp, drain them very well, and serve them quickly. They should be very crisp outside, and nice and runny within. Serves 4.

4

GNOCCHI ALLA ROMANA

These are the ones made with semolina and not with flour as the French ones are. Not only a first-class dish for lunch or supper, but beautiful to look at with its warm tints of brown, and such a grateful change from macaroni cheese!

1 pint milk	1 egg-yolk
5 oz semolina	1½ oz butter
pepper and salt	4 oz *Gruyère* cheese ⎱ or
grated nutmeg	*Parmesan* cheese ⎰ Cheddar

Bring the milk to the boil and sprinkle in the semolina. Season with pepper, salt and grated nutmeg, and cook slowly for twenty minutes, preferably in a double saucepan. Then thicken it with an egg-yolk, and spread it to cool in a layer half an inch thick. When it is cold, stamp it out into rounds of two inches diameter, arrange these in a buttered fireproof dish, sprinkle them with a mixture of grated *Gruyère* and *Parmesan* cheese (or Cheddar would do) and with melted butter, and brown them quickly in the oven. Serves 4.

LENTEN TRIPE

This amusing dish is another substitute for the macaroni cheese of my youth. Like nearly all cheese dishes it is vastly improved by an accompaniment of spinach.

3 oz flour	salt and pepper
2 eggs	¾ pint white sauce
½ pint milk	2 oz cheese

Make a batter with the flour, eggs, and milk, season with salt and pepper, and cook your pancakes. As soon as they are done, roll them up, and cut them across in thinnish strips, piling these up in a dish. Pour over them a thick white sauce, sprinkle with grated cheese, and brown quickly in the oven. Serves 4.

PAPRIKA CHEESE CAKES

These savoury biscuits were the result of a visit to some friends of my sister who lived in a large modern house by a lake near Reading. They were, and are, perfect fare for a picnic or cocktails out-of-doors. The observations on Hungarian paprika on page 14 apply.

2 oz almonds	salt
6 oz butter	1 teaspoon paprika pepper
6 oz flour	1 egg-yolk
5 oz cheese	1 egg

Grind the almonds with their skins on, and work them to a paste with the butter, flour, three ounces of grated cheese, a pinch of salt, the paprika pepper, and the egg-yolk. Roll out to half an inch thick, brush with beaten egg, and sprinkle the little cakes with more grated cheese. Bake for fifteen minutes in a hot oven. Serves 4.

SWEDISH SAVOURY

This mysterious and baffling combination of flavours is the result of a cutting from the old *News Chronicle* many years ago. Ask your friends to guess its constituents.

1–2 eggs	1 anchovy fillet (or 1 teaspoon
1 onion (medium)	anchovy essence)
2 oz butter	4 pieces toast

Hard-boil an egg or two, and chop finely. Mince an onion, not too large, and fry it golden in some butter. Add a chopped anchovy fillet, or a teaspoonful of anchovy essence, mix together, and then add the hard-boiled egg. Cook together for a few minutes, and pile up on your toast. You want to try and get a mixture so that neither onion nor anchovy predominates. Serves 4.

TOURTE FROMAGE

This plain version of a cheese tart earned its rather fancy name from a friend of ours who had enjoyed it so much that she thought it deserved it. It is really much better hot, but a large slice on a picnic, or a midnight raid on the larder is quite rewarding as a cold snack.

6 oz prepared pastry	salt and pepper
¼ lb *Gruyère* cheese	paprika pepper (or cayenne,
1 egg	optional)
1 cup cream	

Make a flan of pastry and bake it 'blind'. When it is cold fill it with the following mixture: beat well together the grated *Gruyère* cheese, egg, and cream. Season with a little salt and pepper and, if you like, a little paprika pepper or a speck or two of cayenne. Bake in the oven for about a quarter of an hour, when the top will be golden and the inside too creamy and delicious for words. Serves 4.

INDEX

INDEX